A Life Worth Living

A Cardiologist's Historical Memoir

Peter Fergus, MD

M&B Global Solutions Inc.
Green Bay, Wisconsin (USA)

A Life Worth Living
A Cardiologist's Historical Memoir

© 2024 Peter A. Fergus

First Edition
All Rights Reserved. The author grants no assignable permission to reproduce for resale or redistribution. This license is limited to the individual purchaser and does not extend to others. Permission to reproduce these materials for any other purpose must be obtained in writing from the publisher except for the use of brief quotations within book chapters.

Disclaimer
In the event you use any of the information in this book for yourself, which is your constitutional right, the author and the publisher assume no responsibility for your actions. Descriptions of treatments, therapies, and life strategies herein come from the experience of the author. It may or may not be appropriate in your case. Talk to your doctor for specific guidance.

All photos are from the Fergus family collection unless otherwise noted.

Front cover: Dr. Peter Fergus shown in 1998 with a heart model used for patient education.

ISBN: 978-1-942731-50-4

Designed and published by M&B Global Solutions Inc.
Green Bay, Wisconsin (USA)

Dedication

*To my parents,
who gave me the genes, the opportunities,
and the determination to succeed ...*

*And to my wife, who gave me the love, support,
and space to keep my focus on the future.*

Contents

1. The Epiphany 1
2. The Arrival of Peter Andrew Fergus 5
3. Antisemitism 11
4. Adventures with Grandma Bertha 19
5. The Buildup to World War II 27
6. André Forgacs in America 37
7. Rita Jeanne Daley 41
8. Personalities 49
9. The Stresses of the Early Twentieth Century 53
10. The Cold War 59
11. The Piano 63
12. The Flute 71
13. Rita's Devotion 79
14. "Bandi" 89
15. Everyday Life 99
16. Religion, Politics, and Hugs 107
17. Nurturing Women 115

Contents

18. Kathy's Childhood Challenges 125
19. Kathy and Peter 135
20. Our college years 143
21. Mrs. Fergus Meets Mrs. Fergus 149
22. Medical School and Beyond 155
23. West Roxbury to Green Bay 167
24. 1975 to 1995 171
25. Green Bay HeartCare 183
26. Changing Healthcare in Green Bay 199
27. The Merger 205
28. The OIG 213
29. Internal Challenges 219
30. Nature, Nurture, and Determination 223
31. Epilogue - Breaking Walls 235
Acknowledgements 241
About the Author 245

Chapter 1

The Epiphany

I had just discharged a patient from the hospital and felt a spring in my step, a sensation not there when I had walked into her room. I heard a background of nurses' voices as I turned and walked down the medical floor at Bellin Memorial Hospital in Green Bay, Wisconsin, to see my next patient. I wasn't listening, as my mind was focused on the realization that in the span of fifteen minutes, I had just convinced an anxious, fearful patient that she was well enough to go home. This was something my partners had been unable to accomplish over three days while I was away.

It was 1984. I was forty years old and had been a cardiologist for ten years. More accurately, I had been "practicing" cardiology for ten years. I use the verb "practice" because we learn medicine by repetitively applying our knowledge-based skills on real patients, not by simply stepping into the coronary care unit. The spring in my step was the result of the realization that all my practicing was actually producing real results. I had seen many forms of heart disease, listened to many descriptions of cardiac symptoms, and converted many sick patients to well ones. Most importantly, I had learned the potent effect that anxiety has in the ability of patients to deal with heart disease. This is why I was successful in convincing my reluctant patient that morning that she was, in fact, ready and well enough to go home.

Did my body language, my words communicate trust, charisma, and compassion? Regardless, something happened to that patient and to me, ending in my distinct feeling, "By George, I think I've got this!"

Practicing medicine is exhilarating, meaningful, and emotionally rewarding. It can be immediately gratifying or frustratingly stubborn in its response to our best efforts. Most importantly, it requires a very real sensitivity to the patient's emotions as well as a close awareness of

Peter Fergus, MD, in 1989

our own emotions as they reflect those of our patients. Those who are normally docile and forgiving may become irritable and demanding when not feeling well, especially if they are wondering if their last day on planet earth might be just around the corner. If a patient's irritability triggers irritability in the physician, then two irritable people do not make for a productive relationship.

I suspect this psychological conflict between my patient and my partners is what led to her refusal to go home those three days prior to my return. As confident as I felt that day, I still realized that I was young and needed more experience with my hands to feel the pulsations of the heart, palpate the size of the liver, and squeeze the swelling of the legs. I needed to expand my mind to integrate the sounds of the heartbeat, the qualities of a heart murmur, the sound of a carotid artery blockage.

And I needed to involve myself more deeply in my own ability to empathize in order to be able to integrate all of this information to a level so reassuring that I could convince my patients that I know what is wrong and how to fix it.

As St. Francis of Assisi put it, "He who works with his hands is a laborer; he who works with his hands and his head is a craftsman; he who works with his hands and his head and his heart is an artist." I had the feeling that I was close to that pinnacle, but I didn't realize how much further I needed to go. Actually, over the next forty years, I have learned what it means to be a true artist according to St. Francis of Assisi – far beyond what I imagined myself to be at that time in 1984.

Knowing, treating, and helping patients over multiple decades rather than multiple months or years gave me access to quicker and more accurate diagnoses, resulting in greater patient confidence in my abilities. That confidence then gave rise to enormous trust, so powerful that I have many patients now who will not make any changes in their medical care without checking with me first, whether it be a change in a prescription medication, a new advertised supplement, a non-cardiac procedure recommended by another doctor, or the safety of a planned vacation. Women ask me about hormone replacement therapy or uterine bleeding with blood thinners; men ask me about medications for erectile dysfunction or prostate problems. Patients come to me with questions arising from misleading soundbites they hear about baby aspirin on television. All these questions come to me even though my business card says only "Cardiovascular Disease."

TRUST. It does not come easily or quickly. It takes time – lots of time – focused on caring, sensitivity, warmth, and empathy, as well as the demonstration that over and over I have made people feel better and, in many cases, returned their lives to normal. Continuing my contacts with patients, seeing them at least once a year or as often as once every two weeks when needed, enables them to see me getting older, but it does not matter. They simply do not want me to retire; they beg me not to retire. Many have never even seen another cardiologist in thirty or forty years.

When they inevitably wind up asking me about retirement, I always respond, "I love what I do, and I have no plans on retiring until I am dragged out of here on a stretcher." How did I get to this level of St. Francis's artistry? Let's start at the beginning: my parents.

Chapter 2

The Arrival of Peter Andrew Fergus

On March 31, 1944, Rita Jeanne Fergus and Andrew Fergus announced the birth of their first child, a boy, Peter Andrew Fergus. It was a simple declarative statement commonly used by new parents. However, this announcement was not completely factual. My father's name was not Andrew Fergus. It was, in fact, André Forgacs. He had changed his name upon arrival in New York City in 1935. He had no clandestine reason for this change. He simply wanted to hide his Jewish heritage. Forgacs is a common Jewish name in his birthplace of Hungary, and this would have immediately marked him as Jewish in his new country, far from Adolf Hitler's influence which was expanding in the early 1930s.

He was grateful to have finally made his way to the United Sates with its opportunities and geographical distance from the prejudice he had previously encountered in Europe. As safe as America appeared on the surface, however, he was not convinced that the potent antisemitism he had seen developing so insidiously around him during his youth could not happen in his new country. His name change thus offered some degree of protection for himself and his future family against local despots who could, in the future, model themselves after Hitler.

In spite of his foreign accent, my father wanted to be regarded as completely American with his new Scottish-sounding name. He quickly became a naturalized citizen, at which time it was easy to transit from André to Andrew, just as the Spanish Pedro easily converts to Peter and the Slovenian Katrina becomes Katherine. The transition from Forgacs was a bit more challenging, but actually made sense because the final portion of his European education in medicine took place at the Royal College of Scotland. He thus had an emotional connection with the country and was familiar with Scottish culture, as well as the frequent use of the name Fergus as both a surname and a given name.

As for his middle name, I was never informed he had one, but I suspect it had Jewish roots. My father felt a middle name was superfluous anyway. He was born in Budapest, Hungary, in 1911, the son of Eugene, a banker, and Bertha, a devoted mother of two sons whom she followed wherever they went as they pursued their studies, passing through several countries in Western Europe. My father desperately wanted to come to the United States to finish his studies, ultimately reaching his goal when he landed in New York City in 1935. He became a naturalized citizen so that he would qualify for joining the US Army, which he ultimately did as a psychiatrist in the early 1940s.

My father, André Forgacs, in 1946 while stationed in Puerto Rico with the US Army

As I grew older, he would tell me and others that the reason behind the name change was no one could spell "Forgacs." While I accepted this explanation initially, it became apparent over the years that there were serious problems with people spelling "Fergus" correctly. I would receive questions like, "Is it Furgis? Or Furgus? Or is it Fergis?" Sometimes "Fergus" would become "Ferguson."

So what had we really gained by the name switch? In a word, nothing! It remained a spelling issue. I did not know the truth about my father's heritage until my sophomore year in high school when my father gave me "the talk." This was not the talk about the "birds and the bees."

Me at age three at the army base in Puerto Rico

This time, "the talk" was about my father being of Jewish heritage. In retrospect, it was not really a surprise to me because my friends would frequently ask if I was Jewish because of my appearance and the fact my father had an elite position as a psychiatrist who had been trained in Europe and spoke with a foreign accent. He was very perceptive about human nature because of his psychiatric training and was fearful that another Jewish purge could occur in this country. Therefore, asked me to keep this information to myself. I did as he asked, and it was not until my wife and I were engaged that I told her. Like my father had done with me, I didn't tell my sons until they were in high school. Thus, we reasoned our safety was secured.

He had lived in Europe during the 1920s and 1930s, when the bigotry and prejudices of Hitler were just germinating. My father was seriously concerned about the Jewish persecution in Nazi Germany, Austria, and Hungary. He had heard about death camps and ultimately the Holocaust. There were descriptions of the beautiful blue Danube River in

Budapest turning red with the blood of Jews who were executed by machine guns on bridges spanning the river.

It is very difficult to get such descriptions out of my mind, especially when my father may have known some of them. As a consequence, he was always afraid of the risk of antisemitism rising in the United States with similar consequences. Sadly, in Charlottesville, Virginia, in 2017, my father's fears came true regarding the early manifestation of antisemitism with marchers chanting, "Jews will not replace us." This chant obliquely referenced the ascendancy of Jews over Gentiles in the German workforce, which was struggling because of the punishing items of the Treaty of Versailles following World War I.

There were approximately two million Jews in Hungary between 1910 and 1920. Although a relatively small number, Jews were concentrated in the elite professions such as banking, commerce, arts, law, and medicine, which created jealousy among the general unemployed population created by the Great Depression which was fostered by the Treaty of Versailles. And now here it was in Charlottesville, Virginia, with the chanted slogan, "Jews will not replace us." Fortunately for my father, he did not have to experience his worst fear. He had passed away in 1985 at the age of seventy-four from congestive heart failure. I'm grateful that my father did not have to see or hear those images or comments.

During the 1920s and 1930s, stimulated by the explosive tirades of Hitler, prejudice against Jews was gradually becoming more frequent. Hitler considered Jews to be of a race that could be purged, but he could find no legal definition of a Jewish race. Therefore, he created a race for Jews by way of the Nuremberg Laws of 1935. These laws proposed a complex formula to determine who was Jewish and who was Christian. It was too easy to classify a person as a Jew simply by the fact that he went to a synagogue. Using such a distinction, those who went to synagogues would be Jews and those who did not would be Gentiles. Therefore, in order to make Judaism more like a racial identity, the Nazis looked at heritage, specifically parents and grandparents and their religious practices.

But as they worked down the genetic ladder, it became very complicated when there were offspring of mixed marriages, a Jew married to a Christian. How those offspring were classified is far too complicated for me to understand, let alone describe. Suffice it to say, there was one item in the Nuremberg Laws that grabbed my father's attention and that was the following: "The offspring of a marriage between a Jew and a non-Jew is considered a Jew." If such a law were to spread to the United States, as it did in every country in Europe conquered by Nazi Germany, my brother, my sister, and I would all be Jews in the eyes of the government. We could be susceptible to the horrors of Nazi Germany-style discrimination, even though we had become confirmed in the Episcopal Church. Hence, the need for the secrecy of our heritage.

At the time of our "talk," I thought my father was worrying too much about antisemitism in America. What happened in Germany could never happen here, I thought. But now in the early twenty-first century, I realized my father was actually prescient. What he feared in his mind during his early years became apparent to me, a generation later, with the display of antisemitic behavior in America brought to life in real time in Charlottesville, and then dramatically escalated in 2023 and 2024 as a result of the Israel-Hamas war.

What I saw years ago – Jews as the playful butt of rather comic comments about their involvement with money – became hostile rhetoric and violent attacks directed at Jews and synagogues. The behavior in Charlottesville conveyed horrific memories of early Nazi Germany; memories now transplanted to the United States.

How I wish that my father were still alive so I could tell him he was correct in his worries — worries which I seriously doubted at the time.

Chapter 3

Antisemitism

Prior to World War I, Austria-Hungary was a land-locked country with multiple neighbors, including portions of Ukraine, Czech Republic, Romania, Italy, Serbia, Moldau, and Montenegro. With so much influence from outside, it is not surprising that many in the country were multilingual, and it explains why my father was fluent in many of the languages which helped him so well in his postgraduate training that took him to a number of western European countries.

Austria-Hungary was a dual monarchy led by a king in each half of the country. It consisted of 52 million people in 1914, 21 million of which were Hungarian. It was a major power in the region. The breakdown of languages within the country at that time were 23% who spoke German, 20% Hungarian, 13% percent Czechoslovakian, 10% Polish, 6% Romanian, 4% Serbian, and 2% Italian.

The capital of the Hungarian sector was Budapest, where my father was born on September 4, 1911. Arriving on this stage only three years before the breakout of World War I on June 28, 1914, he was exposed to the conflicts occurring all around the country. He entered his formative years in the 1920s, which was a time when German aggression was becoming more and more intense. He became progressively more aware of this aggression and its associated eyebrow-raising prejudice against Jews. There were only 2 million Jews in Austria-Hungary in 1940, representing 4.7% of the total population. However, these Jews were in elite economic positions of banking, commerce, arts, law, and medicine, creating a distinct diversity between Jews and common laborers.

This economic diversity was a direct result of the ending of World War I on November 11, 1918, and a reflection of the Paris Peace Accord and the Treaty of Versailles. This treaty led directly to the separation of Austria and Hungary into two separate countries under separate rulers and separate governments. This separation opened the door for Germany, which ultimately took advantage of the political upheaval, to invade and occupy Hungary in 1944.

There was great consternation regarding the Treaty of Versailles, not just in Austria and Hungary, but throughout Europe. There was great unrest within the German population because of the Treaty's punitive penalties and reparation requirements. Under the terms, Germany agreed to pay for a good portion of the damaged property its military had generated during the war. Magnifying this unrest was the Treaty's requirement that Germany accept guilt for starting the war on September 1, 1939, with its invasion of Poland.

Beyond the financial repercussions of the war, Germany was forced to surrender colonies in Africa, Asia, and the Pacific, as well as ceding land to Poland, France, Czechoslovakia, and others. The German army was reduced to 100,000 men; the conscription of new recruits was forbidden; and there was no more construction of armored vehicles, submarines or any other wartime materials. The allied victors of WWI simply wanted to ensure that Germany would never rise to wartime power in the future.

Nevertheless, because of the Allies' focus on "appeasement," Hitler was able to eliminate or ignore all of the guardrails designed to prevent such an outcome, enabling him to create one of the strongest military build-ups in history. The wartime industry that Hitler fostered prior to World War II brought a boom to the German economy, which was much-needed because of the treaty-enforced elimination of its wartime economy in WWI. The previously robust economy prior to World War I had become a bust following the conclusion of the war and the initiation of the provisions of the Treaty. As a result, most of the labor force lost their jobs and were seriously struggling for survival.

Meanwhile, the Jews were functioning very well in the postwar economy, ensconced in the elite professions, not as laborers. Two of these professions focused on money: banking and commerce, thereby linking Jews with money. This, in turn, created strong jealousy and envy among the unemployed laborers who had been relieved of their wartime occupations. In addition to the financial occupations of the Jews, they were very much involved in the financially stable and respected occupations of medicine and the law, as well as the entertainment industry. The dichotomy that occurred between the success of the Jews in the German economy and the failure of the majority of the Gentile population to make a living, let alone find employment, created fertile soil for Hitler's disparagement of Jews in general. As a result, he discovered through his antisemitic diatribes to Hungarians a very willing and responsive population for his opinions, motivated by a compelling undercurrent of jealousy. It was then a short step from jealousy to hatred, with the ultimate goal of Jewish race annihilation.

A more graphic demonstration of antisemitism in Austria-Hungary took place in Vienna, the capital of Austria. However, first I need to step back a few years to 1866 to explain subsequent events. Austria and Hungary were separate countries at the time. The Austro-Prussian War, also known as the Seven Weeks' War, had ended with the defeat of Austria. In response, Austria annexed Hungary the following year to beef up its military force in case of further conflict. Vienna remained the capital of Austria-Hungary, and featured some startling statistics.

Austria-Hungary went progressively downhill following WWI, especially its famous and highly respected capital. Vienna was the home of famous composers during the nineteenth century. They bridged the gap between the classical period of music, with its well-defined compositional structure, and the romantic period, with its focus on music's ability to create pictures and stories. Familiar names such as Ludwig Van Beethoven, Amadeus Mozart, Franz Schubert, and Joseph Hayden were household names in Vienna.

Viennese superlatives actually went far beyond music, making it the cultural center of Europe in literature, philosophy, art, design, medicine, law, and the sciences. To fully understand the contribution of the Jews to this high level of success, consider the following statistics: Vienna's population in 1923 was 201,573; in 1934, the census listed 11% of the Viennese population as Jewish. Out of this 11% of the total population, the practitioners of medicine were 52% Jewish; of banking, 75%; of the law, 85%; of the theater, 63%; and of wine dealers, 74%. All were occupations that were inherently financially very stable.

The dichotomy between this group and the general labor force created a strong underlying bias against the Jews. As result, 130,000 Jews had left Vienna by 1941. The 65,000 who stayed behind eventually were deported to concentration camps, and only about 2,000 survived. It was the end of the golden age of Vienna, which had reached its pinnacle on the shoulders of the Jewish population.

The spread of antisemitism in Austria as a native prejudice rather than an import from Germany is documented by the fact that the mayor of Vienna from 1897 to 1910 was Karl Luger, whose anti-Jewish views were so strong they were highlighted and praised by Adolph Hitler in his diatribe against Jews in his book, *Mein Kampf*, published in 1925. Given that 20% of Hungarians spoke German in the 1920s, it is no surprise that the German hatred of Jews quickly magnified the already established antisemitism extant there for many decades. The very strong native Hungarian antisemitism was brooding there long before Hitler's appearance on the European stage. In fact, the German occupation of Hungary during WWII did not occur until 1944.

After Hungary's separation from Austria following WWI, there were several occasions in the 1930s in which Hungarian authorities murdered greater than 20,000 Jews. There were also deportations of 22,000 Jews from the Subcarpathian region of Hungary, which was acquired from Germany and occupied by many Polish and Soviet Jews. Most of them were deported to neighboring Ukraine, where they were killed. Hungary did ultimately become part of the Axis of power in Europe, but its alliance with Germany was more nuanced than simply becoming ideologically aligned. The leaders of Hungary felt it was safer being friends with Germany rather than its enemy, a sentiment that recalls the old adage, "Keep your friends close, but keep your enemies closer." Alas, this plan turned out to be illusory, as Hungarians saw German soldiers invade and occupy their country in 1944.

Here is a timeline that explains more clearly the relationships between Hungary, Austria, Austria-Hungary, and Germany:

> **Before 1866** – Austria and Hungary are separate countries.
> **1866** – Austria loses the Seven Weeks' Austro-Prussian War.
> **1867** – Austria annexes Hungary to enlarge its military, forming Austria-Hungary.
> **1914** – Germany starts World War I.
> **1918** – Germany loses WWI and is required by the Treaty of Versailles to separate Austria-Hungary into two separate countries with Vienna serving as the capital of Austria and Budapest the capital of Hungary.
> **1934** – Hitler rises to political power and the Allies initiate a program of appeasement toward Germany, which paves the way for Germany's expansion with its attendant antisemitism.
> **1938** – Germany occupies Austria.
> **1944** – Germany occupies Hungary.

I was very interested in foreign languages when I was in junior high school and then high school. When I was in seventh grade, my father hired a Spanish professor from the University of Maine to come to our home to teach my brother and me. This program lasted two years, which allowed me to start my Spanish education in high school at a third-year level. I also studied three years of Latin and three years of French. In the face of my clear interest in foreign languages, I asked my father why he never showed any inclination to teach me Hungarian or at least expose me to a few useful phrases. His response was, "There is nothing good about Hungary." There was no amplification of this opinion, but my further understanding of Hungarian antisemitism amid my ultimate awareness of my father's Jewish heritage spoke volumes.

Hungary passed one of the first antisemitic laws in Europe in 1920, followed by more than 300 anti-Jewish laws and decrees enacted well before Germany entered the country. These laws and decrees led to serious restrictions on Jewish society in Hungary, including restrictions on young Jews entering into the elite professions. There were also prohibitions of non-Jewish individuals from seeking the advice of Jewish lawyers, doctors, and educators. The new decrees even restricted Jews from participating in the entertainment industry, which is an important part of any society that is economically struggling and dealing with depression. These laws and decrees, which were firmly established in the late 1930s, ultimately led to the exodus of millions of Jews from Hungary. Many of those who did not foresee the impending dangers of Jewish persecution were forcibly removed from their homes and transported to other countries sympathetic to the Nazi regime, ultimately becoming victims of the Holocaust.

One of the antisemitic decrees passed in the 1930s had a direct effect on my father and his future educational plans. Matriculation of Jews into the four colleges in Budapest was dramatically reduced from 34% to only 8%. My father could not sit back and see his access to medical education become denied as a result of Jewish hatred and bigotry. Therefore, his family pulled together and decided that my father and his brother, Paul, would travel through Western Europe for their post-secondary school graduate education to include Italy, France, Scotland, and England. Such diverse travel, motivated by the need to access the study of anatomy, physiology, biochemistry, and histology, as well as the opportunity for patient interaction related to psychiatry, surgery,

OB-GYN, and the subspecialties of internal medicine, would not be an easy matter.

Enter Bertha Forgacs. Wherever my father's educational pursuits carried him, his mother was there to feed him, encourage him, and do his laundry. She helped her sons find new apartments so they could focus on achieving the excellence in course work required to climb the ladder toward their goals of practicing medicine. To accomplish these travels, Bertha had to leave her husband, the details of which were never discussed in our family. I was, therefore, left to believe that a mother's love for her children was stronger than her love for her husband. However, being a banker, it is possible that my father's father, Eugene, was captured by the Germans and deported. I will never know.

However, I have a clue that possibly reflects his fate in the form of two rings given to me by my mother after my father's funeral. They had been given to him by Bertha. The first was a gold signet ring with my grandfather's initials, E.F., inscribed on the top. It fit perfectly on my ring finger, suggesting that my grandfather was of similar short stature as my father and me. The second ring was also in gold. Its benign appearance belied the horrifying times in which such a ring was created. It had a plain, flat top with no inscription that could draw any attention to it, thereby hiding its clandestine purpose. The top could be lifted to a 45-degree angle, revealing a short, tubular structure designed to hold a lethal dose of cyanide. The ring's purpose was to offer the Jewish ring bearer the opportunity to immediately end his life in order to avoid, if captured by the Nazis, the torture of being corralled into a railroad cattle car destined to a concentration camp, where death surely awaited him by gas chamber or machine gun. (I subsequently learned that even Winston Churchill had a cyanide capsule secreted in the cap of his fountain pen in case of Nazi capture.)

Some Jews were placed in forced marches, regardless of health or stamina, and herded into neighboring Ukraine, where they also faced certain extermination. The ring offered escape, through immediate death with a semblance of pride, from an ignominious, tortuous end of life at the hands of Nazi criminals. Did my grandmother have the ring because her husband never needed to use it? Did he use it and it was found on his body? Did he offer it to her for her own use if she were ever confronted by Nazis in her travels? Or was it a macabre remembrance of the horrors of the Jewish persecution prevalent at the time and carried on the shoulders of Hitler's rise to power? Whatever, in my hands it was a very sad reflection of the rising fear and panic among the Hungarian Jewish population in the 1930s.

I owe much to my parents and my grandmother, Bertha: from my work ethic, to my personality focused on compassion, empathy, and music. To my father I owe my very existence thanks to his detailed analysis of Hungarian and European politics of the day, his subsequent farewell to the uncertainties of Eastern Europe, and his long-anticipated arrival in New York City in 1935. Of course, my mother had a lot to do with it, too. I must digress and discuss my grandmother first, including the escalating upheavals in Europe that finally enabled my father to convince his mother that the time had come for her to drop anchor in New York City in 1939, only mere months before the breakout of WWII.

Chapter 4

Adventures with Grandma Bertha

Larger than life — three words which serve as a tantalizing introduction to my grandmother, Bertha Forgacs. She was an impish, four-foot eight-inch, 100-pound "magna mater" with an enveloping personality, nerves of steel, and a drive to match any army drill sergeant. She was individually responsible for removing her two sons, André and Paul, from Budapest to Western Europe so they could pursue their postgraduate medical school studies, away from the antisemitic seeds that would, within a decade, grow into the Holocaust.

Bertha left her husband so that she could take care of her two boys. Not only did she finance their education and rent their apartments in each city, from Italy to France to Scotland and then Great Britain, she domestically cared for them by doing their laundry, cooking their meals, buying their groceries, praising their accomplishments, and raising their spirits when struggling. There can be no better demonstration of love than the many interventions she accomplished to help them succeed in their goals to become doctors of medicine.

The three of them living in London in the mid-1930s were well aware

Me, at age two, with Grandma Bertha

of the rise of Adolf Hitler from a wounded soldier in World War I to his ascent to power in the 1920s, culminating in his total control of the National Socialist Party as "the Führer" in 1934. This power progression was fueled by Hitler's personal ambition, his powerful persona, and his dynamic speaking ability. He focused his propaganda on the dangers of the Jewish race, a position already germinating within the population in a jealous hatred of the Jews, who were succeeding in elite professions while the average German laborer was seriously struggling economically.

As a result of Bertha's ability to cover educational expenses as well as lodging and food, her two sons never had to work, enabling them to focus on and succeed in their studies. My father carried that program a generation further by covering my expenses for tuition, room, board, and books while I was in college, and then paying for my medical school tuition and books.

Following the lead of my grandmother and my father, I paid it forward by covering tuition, books, and room and board for my three sons as they pursued their goals in the business world, nursing college, and medical school, respectively. In addition, I established the Andrew Fergus Memorial Scholarship, providing financial help to promising nursing students at Bellin College of Nursing in Green Bay, Wisconsin. As of this writing, this scholarship fund has been helping students for fifteen years and counting.

Bertha's love for her two sons ultimately found its way to me, her first grandson. In return, I loved her and the deep warmth and attention she focused on me, especially when it came to building my knowledge and interest in music and even in medicine. When I was only four years old, my grandmother introduced me to a record album called *Peter and the Wolf*. I loved it and played it over and over again. It involved music and words composed by Sergei Prokofiev, and was based on a Russian folk story about a boy named Peter and his run-in with a wolf who ate Peter's friend, a duck. Prokofiev's motivation to write this music was his desire to introduce the sounds of different orchestral instruments to young children. Most of the sounds were played by individual instruments, but Peter's theme was played by the entire string section of the orchestra.

At that young age, I identified with anybody named Peter, whether the character came from *Peter and the Wolf*, *Peter Pan*, or *Peter Rabbit*, but especially this Peter, who had to deal with a wolf. The music attached to Peter was especially important to me because of its expressive melody created by the string section portraying Peter as happy, optimistic, and comfortable even while misbehaving in his unsanctioned forays outside his backyard garden.

Individual instruments represented the other characters. For example, a flute characterized the bird; an oboe for the duck; a clarinet for the cat; a bassoon for the grandfather; and a dissonant harmony of three French horns for the wolf.

As I look back on the story of *Peter and the Wolf*, I cannot help but see this story as a metaphor for my future life and personality. Before I go any further, here is Prokofiev's story:

Peter is a happy little boy living with his grandfather in a cottage with a garden in the backyard protected by a gate. Peter's grandfather tells him that he is never supposed to leave the garden through the backyard gate because there are wolves out there. However, Peter is curious and sees a possible wonderful world outside, and, therefore, decides to walk through the gate leaving the garden behind. Outside the garden he encounters new friends: a bird, a cat, and a duck. Peter's first challenge outside the gate involves the bird who is easy prey for the cat who views the bird as his next meal. However, Peter, using his head, advises the bird to fly to a higher branch of a nearby tree so that the bird will be beyond the climbing ability of the cat. His next challenge is the appearance of the evil wolf, whose menacing personality is frighteningly portrayed by the French horns, who are playing in a half tone dissonant harmony. Peter advises the bird to stay in one of the high branches and advises the duck to swim to the center of the pond in order to be outside the reach of the wolf. However, the duck becomes curious and ventures too close to the edge of the pond and is swallowed whole by the wolf. Peter then decides to capture the wolf. He comes up with an ingenious idea. He advises the bird to fly around the head of the wolf, thereby distracting the wolf's attention while Peter climbs up onto a tree branch and drops a rope formed into a lasso, catching the wolf by the tail. At this time, three hunters appear with their rifles pointed at the wolf ready to shoot. However, Peter convinces them not to shoot and instead to help him take the wolf to a zoo. As they are headed toward the zoo, Peter hears the duck quacking in the wolf's stomach because he was swallowed whole.

The rest of the story is left to the listener's imagination. As I look back on Prokofiev's story at my current age, I now understand why it resonated so metaphorically for me. With the help of hindsight, here is my present day interpretation:

Peter is a contented little boy who is curious and would like to see what life is like outside the gate (the box). He knows there are other worlds (opportunities) to explore and enjoy. When he met the bird, the cat, and the duck, he was very sensitive to their different personalities, and physical abilities and disabilities (individual analysis). Peter had excellent visual perception as well as emotional perception, and noted the imminent danger facing the bird (anticipating problems). He then wisely advises the bird to escape danger by flying to a higher branch of the nearby tree beyond the reach of the cat. Peter also senses the imminent danger to the duck and encourages the duck to swim to the center of the pond out of reach of the wolf (life-saving advice). However, Peter is dismayed to see the duck failing to follow his instructions, leading to his ingestion by the wolf, a most unhappy result. (Patients don't always follow instructions.)

Peter also demonstrated a creative mind and devised a way to capture the wolf. (Let's rethink this problem.) He advised the bird to distract the wolf while Peter dropped a rope onto the wolf's tail, thereby capturing the wolf and holding him captive (problem resolution). When the hunters arrived with their rifles pointed at the wolf (unexpected complication), Peter takes mercy on the wolf and convinces the hunters to help him take the wolf to the zoo (hospital). On the way to the zoo, Peter hears the duck quacking and knows that where there is speech, there is life (never give up). He also knows that in spite of the evil nature of the wolf, there is goodness in everybody, namely the duck in the wolf's belly (struggling to be treated). Peter knows that when they get to the zoo (hospital), there will be medical care and the duck will be saved. (Crisis averted.)

This analysis shows that Peter was inquisitive, thinking outside the gate (box) in search of new experiences. He analyzes new friends, assessing their strengths and their weaknesses, advising them how to stay alive and avoid the danger of the evil wolf (illness). He also becomes aware of the fact that friends do not always follow instructions and as a result fall into danger. However, when danger arises, there is always a solution. He realizes that even an evil wolf can have goodness within him and is worth saving, which can be done in a zoo (hospital).

Peter's experiences resonated with my DNA at age four and set me on a course, bringing me to where I am today, all the while building the thoughtfulness, creativity, compassion, optimism, and determination introduced to me by little fictional Peter.

Those days were indeed wonderful days for me. I would sit side-by-side with my grandmother, listening to the music and talking about little Peter as I learned about all the sounds of orchestral instruments. Grandma Bertha further advanced my musical education at age eight when she bought for me my first classical album, Beethoven's *Violin Concerto in D major*. It is an emotionally expressive piece of music that was especially appealing to my grandmother, who loved music from the romantic age of the 1800s, when music was composed to represent stories and pictures. That is exactly what the music of *Peter and the Wolf* did for me.

The first movement of the violin concerto begins with four simple tympani taps. All I have to do is imagine those four taps and I can hum the melodies, which are some of the most lyrical melodies of all classical music. I loved it and played the album over and over, which is why Grandma Bertha chose this Beethoven concerto to introduce me to classical music.

Many years later, I have been watching DVDs from *The Great Courses*, which presents college-level lectures on music as well as many other topics ranging from philosophy to religion, from engineering marvels to mathematical tricks. I routinely watch them to stimulate my mind while I walk on the treadmill every morning. During one recent lecture, I was fascinated by Dr. Robert Greenberg, who chose in his course *The Great MasterWorks of Music,* to devote four lectures on the same Beethoven *Violin Concerto* that had so enthralled me when I was only eight years old and has subsequently become fixed in my memory. He took apart the various segments of the first movement and focused on these same four beginning notes. He elaborated on their significance by pointing out how Beethoven used these four notes over and over, acting as a bridge to connect his multiple melodies to create a cohesive whole, uniting their variations by the orchestra as well as the violin soloist. In my naive young mind, I was only aware of the four introductory taps, but they persist, even now in my eighties. Tthey were literally "drummed" into my brain by Beethoven's repetitive use of these four tympani taps to create one of the most beautiful violin concertos ever written.

My entry into the study of medicine occurred at the age of eight, also courtesy of Grandma Bertha when she took me on my first visit to the public library. She encouraged me to take out a biography of Louis Pasteur, which I understood and thoroughly enjoyed reading as my introduction to bacteria. Bertha's self-confidence, which powered her through the hostilities of pre-World War II Eastern Europe, was now being generated in me during my early years. Meanwhile, I started taking piano lessons when I was six years old and still remember my first recital when I played Franz Schubert's *The Happy Farmer* in an abridged form for children.

As I compare my sensitivity and drive to my grandmother's, I am sure there is a genetic link because I knew nothing of her European challenges until I was much older. As strong as my grandmother was, I discovered at age six that her personal challenges were not over. A lot of her power found diminishing returns when she came face-to-face with my mother, who was equally driven and uncompromising. I experienced an inkling of the competition between the two of them when I was sitting in the living room, excitedly awaiting the arrival of my grandmother. I was telling my mother how happy I was that I was going to be spending time with Grandma Bertha. My mother responded by telling me not to spend so much time with her because my friends from school would miss me.

Being independent-minded, like *Peter and the Wolf*, I, of course, spent all the time I wanted with my grandmother. I knew my friends would still be there when my grandmother left and my interaction with her was simply too important for me to abbreviate.

Chapter 5

The Buildup to World War II

I always knew it was my father's unceasing persuasion that led to my grandmother's decision to leave her son, Paul, in London and join my father in New York City. Not until my father's revelation of our Jewish ancestry and my subsequent historical awareness of the events preceding World War II did I realize that my father's motivation to convince his mother to leave Europe was a reflection of near panic. He likely thought about his mother, a single woman, a Jew living in a region of the world at extreme danger of being overrun by antisemitism with its horrific potential.

The choice in 1939 for her to move, therefore, was not an arbitrary or whimsical decision. My father, in fact, had wanted her to make the move much sooner. He was an avid reader of the *New York Times* and was well aware of the weakness and ultimate failure of the British policy of appeasement. As soon as he digested the draconian measures of the Treaty of Versailles and their subsequent psychological effects on the German population, he easily came to the conclusion that there would be more than one "Great War," forever to be replaced as a new set called World War I and World War II.

The Treaty of Versailles was signed on June 28, 1919, when my father was only eight years old. He became well aware of the economic and political fallout arising from the treaty during his formative years in high school, including Germany's depression and the rising anger of the German populace. Furthermore, being Jewish, he became well aware of two fundamental interlocking atrocities that were brewing: first, jealousy toward the German Jewish population over their well-paying professional jobs expressed itself in the form of antisemitism among the under-employed German population who were unable to successfully make a living. Second, this frustrated, angry, poverty-stricken German population had created the perfect platform for a ruthless demagogue such as Adolf Hitler to take control of the country, and in the process put into action all of his ideology expressed in *Mein Kampf*, published in 1925-26. Because of Hitler's rhetorical skills, he was able to channel the anger of the common German laborer into a motivating force against all the countries who, through the Treaty of Versailles, forced the restrictive limitations on Germany's economy. On top of that, Hitler was able to funnel his already strong personal antisemitism into a hateful, murderous form dedicated toward Jewish extinction, thereby raising the simmering antisemitic tendencies of the general population to a whole new level.

The allied countries, especially Great Britain, were closely following Hitler's rise from injured soldier in World War I to the Führer of the Nazi party in 1934. My father also was acutely aware of all these developments taking place during his graduate medical education in Western Europe during the early 1930s. It was no coincidence that in 1935, just one year after Hitler became the Fuhrer of Nazi Germany, my father passed through immigration on Ellis Island and landed safely in New York City. He then turned his attention toward getting his brother and mother out of England and into the United States. They, however, were not as prescient regarding the dangers of antisemitism, Hitler, and the rising potential for World War II.

After his arrival in New York, my father became well aware of the isolationist policies that Congress shared with ninety-five percent of the American population regarding the disruption in Eastern Europe. The conflicts were just too far away and the early tales of the fate of German Jews were viewed as exaggerations. In addition, the US was still struggling to come out of the Great Depression, and the last thing unemployed Americans wanted was immigrants vying for jobs here. As a result, the government directed all US consulates in Europe to limit immigration visas to ten percent of their previous levels.

The possibility of Bertha being denied a visa was my father's ultimate argument in prompting her to make the journey to New York. It had taken four years of trying to convince her of the dangers lurking in Great Britain, seemingly far away from the chaos building in Germany, to make the voyage. He never was successful in convincing his brother to leave. Paul preferred instead to study lung diseases and become a staff pulmonologist at Guys Hospital in London.

Meanwhile, Hitler was on a mission through the late 1930s to recover all that Germany had lost by way of the Treaty of Versailles. During his early moves in this direction, the allied countries were in desperate need of some type of policy to reign in Hitler's aggressive rhetoric and expansive military plans, desperation which led to the ill-fated policy of appeasement. In simple terms, "appeasement" means giving an opponent some of what they want in the hope they will be satisfied and not ask for more.

The motivation toward appeasement had three founding principles. First, and foremost, was World War I, called at the time the Great War. The loss of life in the millions, the brutality of advanced military equipment, and the extreme loss of property could not be allowed to repeat itself. Second, the victors of WWI, having experienced such property devastation, did not have the money to rebuild their own military. And third, there was a large group of victorious countrymen throughout Europe who shamefully felt the provisions of the Treaty of Versailles were too punitive, including the restriction of Germany's army to no more than 100,000 soldiers, the prohibition of inscription of new soldiers, and the closure of factories which had thrived during the war through the manufacture of military equipment.

In addition, the treaty had stripped away militarily strategic strips of land from Germany to make sure it would never again be able to plunder its neighboring countries with strong fighting forces. There was a high level of guilt among these appeasers for their role in contributing to Germany's depression through what they viewed as excessively harsh provisions of the treaty. Therefore, when Hitler promoted and compiled the strongest military force of that time, the appeasers, led by Great Britain, turned a blind eye.

"Maybe this military buildup will satisfy him and keep him at peace," they thought.

What they failed to realize, however, was how badly Hitler wanted back the strips of land that Germany had lost through the Treaty of Versailles. Furthermore, they did not realize Hitler's plan for emergence from the depression was to expand Germany's borders and its working taxpaying population. Franklin Delano Roosevelt succinctly described appeasement gone wrong in a fireside chat on December 29, 1940, when he stated, "There is no appeasement with ruthlessness." By the time FDR made this statement, it was abundantly clear that Hitler's expansive goals, his drive and determination, his powerful rhetoric, and his practice of atrocities had been grossly underestimated and would never yield to appeasement.

FDR went on to say, "No man can tame a tiger into a kitten by stroking it. There can be no reasoning with an incendiary bomb."

With all of the above as preamble, the following describes the events which led Bertha to leave Europe and drop anchor in New York City on board the HMS Queen Mary.

Once Hitler's military was established and his war machinery fully deployed, his next concern was how to make use of all this power. His subsequent decisions directly reflected the failure of the appeasement policies of Great Britain, and less so of France, when set against the ruthlessness of a sociopath. Hitler's first goal was to reclaim for Germany the three strips of land which the Treaty of Versailles had removed from Germany's control: the Saarland, the Rhineland, and the Czechoslovakian Sudetenland. The Saarland was Germany's smallest state, tucked into the southwestern part of the country. It may have been a small piece of land, but it had enormous implications when it came to industrialization in regard to coal production and iron manufacturing. Because of the important military value of these products for the creation of Germany's military machine, the Treaty of Versailles had wanted to make sure that Germany never had access to or control over this region again. Therefore, the treaty gave the Saarland to the League of Nations, which had been created by President Woodrow Wilson at the end of WWI.

Of course, Hitler wanted this industrialized region back under Germany's control so he could supply his new war machine. As a result of his determination to regain this small but highly desirable strip of land, he was able to take it back easily with only 20,000 soldiers and virtually no resistance. Ninety percent of the Saarland's population spoke German and actually wanted to be back under the German flag, not stuck in some form of "Never-Never Land" in the League of Nations. The Allies' appeasement policy meant there was no pushback to Hitler's defiance of the Treaty of Versailles. "Let him have it and he'll go away," was their hope.

Hitler then turned his attention to the Rhineland, a segment along the western border of Germany just north of the Saarland. It was another strip of land taken by the Treaty of Versailles, this time to create a demilitarized zone to prevent German forces from expanding into the neighboring countries of Belgium, Luxembourg, Holland, and France. It was no secret that Hitler wanted the Rhineland back in order to create an entry into the occupation of these countries, not only to expand Germany's territory, but also to expand the extreme antisemitic ideas that he harbored. In view of the easy annexation of the Saarland, Hitler simply invaded and took over the Rhineland one year after he reacquired the Saarland, again with very little resistance.

A recurring theme during this period of appeasement was the feeling by many Allied countries that although Hitler's transgressions of the

Treaty of Versailles were illegal, they were acceptable because they were not worth going to war over. The memories of the death and destruction of the Great War were still so very strong. With the fall of the Rhineland, Hitler now had unobstructed access to all of the above-named countries. He did not take advantage of this opportunity, however, until May 1940, because he first had unfinished business in eastern Germany involving another strip of land, this time in Czechoslovakia called the Sudetenland. In view of the fact that Germany had occupied Austria in March 1939, it was not a stretch of the imagination to conclude that he would soon want nearby Czechoslovakia and Poland under his control.

These fears led to the Munich Agreement signed by Germany, Great Britain, France, and Italy (another axis country sympathetic to Germany). British Prime Minister Neville Chamberlain's proposal was a classic example of appeasement. To prevent Hitler from occupying all of Czechoslovakia, Great Britain was willing to give him the strip of land called the Sudetenland, mostly German-speaking people of German culture, provided he did not deport people of Czechoslovakian culture. Hitler also promised not to annex all of Czechoslovakia or any other Eastern European country without prior negotiations. The Munich Agreement was signed, Hitler was satisfied, and Chamberlain was joyously welcomed home to Great Britain with a parade. War had been averted by appeasement. A little strip of land had been given back to Hitler (Who cares?) in exchange for no further encroachment on other countries' territories (War averted).

However, the anti-appeasers were not jubilant because they recognized that the Munich Agreement was not a treaty, not a formal multiparty commitment. There were no guardrails, no penalties for any transgressions from the agreement. Winston Churchill was the strongest politician against appeasement in general, and the Munich Agreement in particular. Indeed, Churchill was correct. Only six months after the Munich Agreement was signed on September 30, 1938, Hitler broke through the absent guardrails and invaded the rest of Czechoslovakia on March 10, 1939, and then Poland on September 1, 1939.

The fracture of the Munich Agreement carried immense implications. Appeasement was not going to work when dealing with a sociopath like Hitler who would do whatever he wanted, especially if there were no consequences. As a result, there was only one conclusion: appeasement was dead. Hitler's subsequent invasion of Poland carried even more immense implications. It was not just the annexation of another country, it was actually the start of World War II, because earlier Poland had signed an agreement with Great Britain and France stating they would come to the defense of Poland in the event of a German invasion. Appeasement was dead. Peace was gone. Great Britain, France, Poland, and Germany were all at war. Neville Chamberlain was out. Churchill was elected prime minister, and Great Britain was now on a war trajectory.

To make matters worse, Hitler was not finished. As previously feared when he took back the demilitarized zone of the Rhineland, he went on to invade Norway and Denmark in April 1940; Belgium, Luxembourg, and the Netherlands in May 1940; and France in June 1940. The Western European allies were left with chagrin and fear, while shamefully marveling over this most impressive series of events that saw Hitler's rapid military buildup and his expansion of Germany's borders.

My grandmother, Bertha, left England just in the nick of time. It was only six months before Great Britain and France declared war on Germany following the invasion of Poland. Even though the initiation of war occurred after Bertha's departure from London, the handwriting was clearly on the wall since the occupation of the Saarland in 1935, the year my father left London himself. He had been well aware of the impending likelihood of Hitler's expansion into the countries west of Germany, beginning with France, which then placed Great Britain in extreme danger across the English Channel.

In addition, my father could not help but be impressed by the futility of the Munich Agreement and the ill-advised policy of appeasement which clearly had failed. He also knew that when France fell, Great Britain, where Bertha was living, would be the only allied country left to do battle with Germany. I'm sure it was with tremendous relief when he saw his devoted mother walking down the gangplank of the Queen

Mary in New York City, his many years of persuasion finally consummated.

Despite the fact Bertha left England only a few months before the German bombing of London (the Blitz), which began September 7, 1940, and continued until May 1941, there were never any discussions of this close call with me by her or my father, even after "the talk" with me about my Jewish heritage in junior high school. There was no point in them reliving the horrors of these bombings, which killed an estimated 40,000 British citizens.

After Bertha's arrival in New York City, one of her first priorities was the disposition of the money she had been carrying with her through Western Europe and across the Atlantic. She explored multiple possibilities for banking institutions in search of safekeeping for her money, and settled on the Bank of New York in New York City for two reasons. First, it was the oldest operating bank in New York City, having been in operation since 1784. Second, she had done her homework in preparation for becoming a naturalized citizen of the United States, and was aware of the fact that Alexander Hamilton, a future secretary of the treasury, had participated in the founding of this bank. Bertha felt very reassured that her money would be safe.

When I think of my little grandmother walking into the large lobby of the Bank of New York, I cannot help but imagine the image of this diminutive lady, carrying her ever-present oversized black purse, and presenting a most-determined expression. She knew what she wanted and was determined to get it. I can picture the banker awaiting her arrival, looking down at his appointment calendar and seeing the name, Bertha Forgacs. During World War I, the German military had developed the largest howitzer at the time, which came to be called "Big Bertha." Since that time, the name Bertha has come to be synonymous with something large, from weapons to university marching bands with their eight-foot diameter base drums. We could almost fit two Grandma Berthas, end-to-end, inside one of these drums!

So here comes Grandma Bertha, all four feet, eight inches, 100 pounds of her. Not only would the banker have been surprised by the incongruity of her name with her appearance, but also the determined, no-nonsense expression on her face. And let's not overlook her Hungarian accent! I doubt very much there was any small talk, because the banker surely would have been nonplussed by her appearance and readiness to negotiate. Furthermore, Bertha was fixed on her goal, which was to invest much of her money in the major American corporations whose stock prices had been driven down by the previous depression. She was financially smart and always self-supporting, including her travels by train and bus in the United States as well as maintaining, for a time, an apartment in St. Petersburg, Florida. I never saw her request or receive any money from my father. Instead, she was the generous one, giving me $1,000 to help me with the down payment on a small home in Brockton, Massachusetts, a forty-five-minute commute to my internship at Boston City Hospital in July 1970.

Chapter 6

André Forgacs in America

My father, André Forgacs, was overjoyed to be in America, a country he had hoped to enter for many years. He envisioned no antisemitism, no vestiges of Hitler's distortion of reality. At long last, he had the opportunity to become a United States citizen. It did not take him long to learn the basics of American history, because this knowledge had already been present in his mind for many years as he would dream about one day arriving in New York City.

He was able to quickly become a naturalized citizen, the certificate he received being forever a treasure in his library. He then passed the official medical examination, called the ECFMG, required of all medical physicians trained in foreign countries before they are allowed to practice medicine in the United States. Passing this examination enabled him to become an intern and resident in medicine in Brooklyn. He then moved to Binghamton, New York, to pursue his interest in psychiatry at the state hospital there. He not only became trained in psychiatry and neurology, but also fell in love with my mother, Rita Jeanne Daley, a nursing student in psychiatry.

At this point, he proudly joined the United States Army with the goal of doing something, anything to get back at the Germans and Hitler for their hatred of not only Jews, but also anyone who did not share their aggressive ideology. Making an impact was a very high priority in his mind.

Grandma Bertha joined my father in Binghamton about a year later. After being responsible for his past, she still felt a very strong pull to be responsible for his present and his future. She settled down very comfortably, renting an apartment and acquiring a German Shepherd mix named Jill, whom she loved and treated as another child. My father, armed with his medical degree and his commission as an army captain, next moved to Canandaigua, New York, to work at the Veterans Administration (VA) hospital there and further his psychiatric training.

During the seven years from 1935 and 1942, he accomplished many landmark goals: passing the ECFMG, getting his medical license to practice medicine, changing his name, becoming a naturalized United States citizen, joining the United States Army, completing his internship and residency in psychiatry, and then marrying my mother in 1942. I joined the family in 1944 followed by my brother, Paul, eighteen months later. Our sister, Patricia, completed our family unit in 1949. Grandma Bertha was a frequent participant as well as a competitor versus my mother in a conflict directed at my father's attention.

Next, his army enlistment transported him to a base in Puerto Rico where he cared for soldiers suffering from "shell shock," which is now called post-traumatic stress disorder or PTSD. My life in Puerto Rico was pretty nice, as evidenced by pictures of my father holding my brother and me in a very nice-looking swimming pool, setting aside the tears on my face from my fear of water at that age. Our living quarters may not have been quite so nice, because I recall living in a Quonset hut, which is an all-purpose, lightweight steel structure with a rounded roof.

The three Fergus kids pose in our favorite cowboy outfits in 1951 in Canandaigua, New York. From left, Peter, Pat and Paul. My favorite cowboy character was Hopalong Cassidy.

There is much to be said about each of these stops during my father's early years in America: the people, the personalities, and the events. Let's began with my mother, the second most important woman in his life, coming, of course, after the awe-inspiring contributions of Grandma Bertha, who had guided him through his medical studies in Western Europe. She loomed as large as her name in his medical school successes. It is no giant leap to sense a fair degree of tension between these two women, who focused their attention and love on the same man.

Chapter 7

Rita Jeanne Daley

When we are young, we have minds like sponges. Life's multiple events fall into our developing brains and find fertile soil for substantial growth. These stimuli determine whom we will love, what we love, how we love, what excites us, and what does not. As important as these events are, they are equally balanced by the messengers who bring them to our attention as we progress from infancy to adulthood. Such a messenger was my mother, Rita. She was a lady of British-Irish descent, a strong Catholic, an equally strong character, and held a determined devotion to make each of her children the best of the Fergus breed.

Beyond her single-minded devotion to my father and their three children lay a complicated woman who never dreamt in her youth that she would become entangled in religious geopolitics, including antisemitism as well as the cultural obstacles created by a German warmonger. Hitler's evil power grew directly from the repressive elements of the

Treaty of Versailles, further colored by his drive to purify the genetics of his German culture by creating a master Aryan race of white, blonde, blue-eyed non-Jewish citizens.

Since our messengers, like my mother, are formed and nurtured by their own influencers and experiences, I must preface my description with an analysis of the cast of characters who molded and encouraged her to become such an immense source of guidance during my formative years.

I will begin with my maternal grandfather, Franklin Daley, known to all of his grandchildren as "Pop." If God ever needed a human model to help him create the prototypical, single-minded, unswayable image of a "majordomo," it was Franklin. In his mind, he was indeed the headmaster and chief steward of the Daley family. He had a large body to support the power and volume of his drill sergeant voice. He had the unflappable, undeniable self-determination that life and all of its consequences were truly his way or the highway. There was no room for compromise because he was Mr. Always Right.

The only softness I could ever glean from him was his piano playing, but even that came with a caveat. His skill was of his own making, because he had the native ability to play the piano by ear, pulling forth harmonics and melody without the ability to read music. He could improvise and add lyrics, but had no interest in, or regard for, classical music and only a vague knowledge of classical composers.

As the fates would ordain it, my musical interest and abilities were completely opposite to his. I was already reading music while playing and memorizing Beethoven and Bach when I was only eight years old. On occasion, I would sit next to him on the piano bench and play one of my pieces for him. Instead of recognizing or even complementing me on my talent, he would try to convert me into playing his kind of music and doing it his way with chords and melody. His musical interests were along the lines of Bing Crosby, Frank Sinatra, and Tony Bennett. I must admit, I wish I had some of his spontaneous piano performance ability, but the genetic strength arising from my father's and grandmother's devotion to classical music, note reading, and emotional expression were just too strong in me.

Franklin was a devout, lifelong Catholic, a family man with a quick temper. It should require no leap of logic to conclude that he had no interest in what was going on in Europe, no interest in Hitler's rising power, and no interest in the purge of the Jewish population in Germany. His attitude is not surprising because, in general, the United States's foreign policy in the 1930s was one of isolation. The memory of the Great War with its seven-digit casualties was fresh in everyone's mind and certainly did not escape Franklin. The feeling of the United States populace was to regard the conflicts developing around Germany as European problems, thousands of miles away and of no personal importance to the average American.

Meanwhile, my father was acutely aware of all the atrocities against the Jews taking place in Europe by way of his close reading of European newspapers when he lived there and later, once he arrived in New York City, multiple American newspapers. Franklin focused on the local Binghamton newspaper, which very likely mentioned only in passing the turmoil in Europe, instead focusing on local New York State conflicts and politics. There is no doubt he knew nothing and cared even less about young white German men who were drafted to become aggressive, hostile, and in a word "mean" men designated to become Stormtroopers. These individuals were highly opinionated, believing that they and their type should and would control the world and all agencies within it. They were not required to be smart, just aggressive and determined to succeed in their goals.

The German code word for their ultimate goal was the "purification" of German culture by creating the "Aryan Race," with no place for minorities from any other race. Such issues were completely lost on my mother's domineering father. It is likely that Franklin was not only ignorant of geopolitics, but also had no sympathy toward foreign individuals who had immigrated from France, England, Ireland, Italy, or Hungary to the United States. The last thing he would have wanted was for a foreigner to enter the United States and attempt to persuade Americans to be sympathetic to Europe's turmoil, which could stimulate America to be drawn into a second world war. In short, Franklin's view of Europe featured neither interest nor sympathy.

On the other end of the personality spectrum were my mother's two sisters, older Reba and younger Flossie. Reba was delightful to be around. She was humorous, easy-going, and most importantly, made the best chocolate fudge in the world, especially when it failed to solidify and turned out as chocolate soup! The failure of such batches of fudge became the standard for chocolate excellence in my mind to this day.

My fondest memory of Reba occurred when she came to New York City from her home in Paterson, New Jersey, to meet with my girlfriend and future wife, Kathy, in the audience at Carnegie Hall to watch the Harvard Band play on the stage. I was a junior at Harvard and second chair flutist in the Harvard Concert Band. We had been invited, along with other Ivy League bands, to play on that venerable stage. I recall looking up from the stage at what seemed like six layers of balconies looking down on us, the same balconies that made my father dizzy when he was walking down the steps to his seat for a concert of classical music many decades earlier. He did not enjoy heights.

My mother's younger sister, Flossie, was the opposite of Reba, making human bookends of opposites between whom was my mother with a personality of a more moderate style. Flossie was shy and quiet, easily unnoticed in a group. She was warm and kind. She and her husband, Neal, lived in a suburb of Binghamton with their two children, Coleen and Timothy. Our contacts were few, and therefore, I have a large vacuum in my memory regarding their family. Nevertheless, I have great fondness for Flossie originating from a picture of St. Peter, given to my mother for Christmas 1944, on the back of which was inscribed my name and birthday, March 31, 1944. Jesus's apostles were very important to Flossie because of her deep Catholic devotion.

I never knew my mother's mother, who passed away when I was only a toddler. All I remember was the cause of her death being a serious illness. Franklin remarried quite a few years later to a woman named May. She was warm and kindly, one you would never expect to be cou-

My mother, Rita (right), poses with her two sisters, Reba (left) and Flossie (center), in 1977.

pled with the fiery, opinionated, and at times explosive Franklin. My only recollection of her is a lobster dinner at our rented summer cottage on Green Lake in Maine in the mid-1950s.

Now that I have described my mother's family, I would like to describe the following scene: A domineering father, a devout Catholic with little or no tolerance for other religions, especially Judaism, no tolerance for foreigners who could attempt to challenge the isolationist policy of the United States, a father now coupled with his favorite and obedient daughter, Rita, who had just indicated that she had fallen in love with a doctor at the state hospital. This doctor was a Hungarian with accented speech, and let's not forget, Jewish. Now imagine these two men standing front and center in my mother's life as she was working her way through nursing school on her way to becoming a psychiatric registered nurse.

On one side was her lover, my father: smart, intellectual, cultured, worldly, empathetic, sensitive, soft-spoken with Hungarian-accented English. On the other side, there was Franklin, my mother's father: brash, opinionated, domineering, loud, uncultured, narcissistic, insular, and bigoted with speech tinged with a New York accent. I think even the Hallmark channel writers would have had a hard time coming up with a happy ending for this complex mix. One possible Hallmark solution might have had Pop converting from Catholicism to Judaism? No way! My father converting from Judaism to Catholicism? Not on your life! Arranging a large wedding reception with sufficient diversity of the guests to convince Franklin to embrace diversity in general? Nope!

My mother, Rita, as a young woman

Instead, my mother rallied her rebellious spirit and, step-by-step, moved toward her goal of marriage. Her first step was not planned, but worked to her advantage by creating a time slot for her major move. Smoking was strictly forbidden at her nursing school. Therefore, she was suspended for a semester after being caught with cigarettes, an example of her rebellious spirit.

Now, what to do with an open schedule while idling with your loved one nearby, you ask? Rita and Andrew took matters into their own hands and eloped in 1942! Who needs father's blessing? In spite of this demonstration of independence, my mother maintained a good relationship with Franklin and visited Binghamton with my brother and me a number of times.

However, I cannot say the same thing about my father and Franklin. I vaguely recall hearing about a face-to-face visit between my parents and Franklin two years later in 1944, a meeting which was not pleasant. Franklin's antipathy may have been muted somewhat by his wife's illness around that same time, but I do not recall ever seeing my father and Franklin together after I became part of the family except for that lobster dinner in Maine. I suspect the original meeting between the two was orchestrated by my mother with the goal of allowing each one to see what the other looked like, importantly reinforced by her pride in displaying her handsome new husband. She undoubtedly also was making an attempt to create some degree of stability between the two of them. However, the striking separation of their personalities made any rapprochement impossible.

I don't think my father ever forgave Franklin for his blatant prejudice against foreigners in general and Jews in particular. In addition, Franklin's isolationist political position for the war threatening in Europe made any coming to terms between the two of them virtually impossible. Franklin certainly was not alone in his opinions. The tendency toward isolationism as a political policy in this country was widespread and firmly embraced. In addition, there was a simmering antisemitic prejudice in the United States, downplaying pro-Jewish sentiment until after the horrors of the Holocaust became well-known.

So how did my mother come up with the sufficiently rebellious spirit to blatantly deny her domineering father's wishes? What kind of personality enables a person to be so determined and so courageous? These questions lead to a discussion of personality traits in general, followed by my mother's individual traits.

Chapter 8

Personalities

As Andrew Fergus became a reluctant member – save for one person – of the Daley family, so began a singular love story challenged by multiple obstacles: personal, familial, and geopolitical. How my mother dealt with these challenges requires an understanding of personality traits, which is the subject of this chapter.

Psychologists recognize five individual personality traits:
- Extroversion
- Agreeableness
- Openness
- Emotional stability
- Conscientiousness

Each trait can be broken down on a scale ranging from low to high. For example, individuals who score high in **Extroversion** are more assertive and dominant, more energetic and active, more upbeat and cheerful, more responsive to rewards, and behave in ways that promote their own happiness.

Individuals who score high in **Agreeableness** generally have a more positive orientation to other people. They are kind, pleasant, sympathetic, helpful, more trusting, and they strive to solve conflicts in ways acceptable to everyone involved. They are more cooperative than competitive, more empathetic than isolated, more able to tolerate frustrations and maintain longer interpersonal relationships.

Persons who score high in **Openness** are more receptive, less dogmatic, more open to new ideas and experiences. They are flexible and not concerned about doing things in a certain way just because that's the way they have always been done. They have fewer conflicts and are less likely to be prejudiced. They maintain relationships that are more than satisfying, get along with others, and are more liked by others. They have more aesthetic sensitivity to art and music including "goosebumps" when exposed to beautiful, expressive music. They also tend to be outgoing, friendly, energetic, organized, and compassionate.

Emotional stability refers to how individuals experience negative emotions. Those scoring low are more likely to overreact to minor conflicts, become "bent out of shape" more easily, are less satisfied in general with their lives, tend to rely on others for emotional support, and in the extreme are needy and dependent. In general, they are less satisfied with their marriages and are more volatile in their close relationships. They are shy, nonassertive, and self-conscious, more likely to see the negative side of opportunities, and more likely to have health issues. They often see challenges as hopelessly difficult.

People who are high in **Conscientiousness** are responsible, dependable, orderly, organized, industrious, and persistent. They make themselves do what needs to be done and show attentiveness to others in need. They are on time, work hard, follow rules, and are highly self-controlled as well as self-disciplined. They typically maintain long social relationships and do what's necessary to maintain good health regardless of the effort required. They are strongly motivated to do anything well, avoiding any distractions.

My mother scored very high in extroversion, agreeableness, openness, and conscientiousness, and extremely high in emotional stability. Her high extroversion and agreeableness scores would predict that she would embrace a new lover far differently from her native Catholicism, and her father's bigotry and provincialism. Her openness gave her the willingness to engage with a foreigner and the emotional strength to understand a man far different from any she had previously encountered. In addition, she had the emotional fortitude to pursue such a relationship with the knowledge of her father's ultimate disapproval.

Her conscientiousness gave her the self-confidence to know, one way or another, she was going to make this new relationship work no matter what details arose from challenges derived from her father. Meanwhile, her emotional stability score was extremely high, enabling her to avoid overreacting to her father's negativity or the unique aspects of a relationship involving a foreigner with a Jewish heritage. Negative thoughts were inconsequential and completely overshadowed by her eternal optimism.

These personality traits are not unique to my mother and were also evident in my grandmother, Bertha, and my father, whom I will describe later. These traits will also be obvious in my descriptions of my wife and the burdens she had to overcome as she grew into adulthood. I, too, reflect these same personality traits in regard to my efforts to blaze multiple trails for the practice of cardiology never before seen in Green Bay, Wisconsin.

Yes, we all ranked high in the positive traits described above. People who rank high in these traits can be summarized as warm, sensitive, empathetic, determined, organized, loving, non-prejudicial, forward-focused, and goal-oriented. With these characteristics circulating in the DNA of the Forgacs/Fergus family, it is therefore no wonder that within this one family are a psychiatrist, a psychiatric nurse, two cardiologists (myself and my son, Todd), a nurse practitioner (my son, Mark), a human resource manager (my son, Scott), a psychologist (my sister, Patricia), and an internist (my brother, Paul).

And let's not forget Grandma Bertha, who did not seek a profession in healthcare, but still scored high in all the above personality traits. This propelled her to travel faithfully throughout Europe with her sons, André and Paul (a future pulmonologist), making sure their personalities were ripe for flourishing in their efforts toward caring, compassionate, conscientious, and agreeable physicians. Bertha and my mother did not share any DNA, but they did share the openness to take on new familial challenges and provide the necessary support to allow their children to prosper and share the benefits of their personality traits with others.

Chapter 9

The Stresses of the Early Twentieth Century

In addition to the personality traits of the individual members of the Fergus family, the family itself had its own personality in the form of a corporate structure. Without question, my father was the chief executive officer (CEO) of the organization. He made all the major life-changing decisions: where we would live, how we would live, who would live with us (that is Grandma Bertha), and how the money would be spent and invested.

His path to the practice of psychiatry began when he responded to a classified ad in a medical journal looking for a psychiatrist to run a private psychiatric hospital in Bangor, Maine. He went by himself to Bangor, evaluated the city of 38,000 people, interviewed for the position, and assessed the hospital. He was impressed, and the hospital owners were impressed with him, especially because he had a foreign accent reminiscent of Sigmund Freud, who was very popular in the 1950s.

My father discussed the details of the opportunity with my mother by telephone and then traveled around the city looking at places to live. He found a 2,000-square-foot house across the street from an elementary school, which became my home until I graduated from high school in 1962. It was a modest, unimposing home with three bedrooms (soon to become four after remodeling an attic space for my bedroom), one bathroom (soon to be remodeled into two after conversion of an upstairs closet into a bathroom for Grandma Bertha), a music room for a baby grand piano, a study for my father's home office, a basement for a future pool table and ping-pong table, as well as a single garage to which was added a carport and a basketball hoop two years later.

In order to obtain financial backing to start his practice, my father went to Minot, North Dakota, to discuss his new opportunity with a close friend from Hungary, who was an established internist in that city. He borrowed $5,000 ($50,000 in 2024 money) to finance the initiation of his practice. He repaid the loan after only one year, confirming the wisdom of the well-researched risk that he took in moving his family to Bangor, a city completely unknown to him until he saw that classified ad for a psychiatrist. His money was well-spent, quickly enabling him to expand his reputation as the only psychiatrist north of Portland, even extending northward more than 300 miles to the Maine-Canadian border.

My mother, on the other hand, was the family's chief operating officer (COO), responsible for taking my father's decisions and turning them into actions for the benefit of the whole family. As a result of my father's required daily absences, I became very close to my mother, who was always home when I returned from school. She was the recipient of a regular summary of my daily events including my study experiences, friends, successes, and disappointments. I knew she would share all the important topics with my father after he arrived home. I shared a lot of information with my mother regarding my friends, to the point that oftentimes my friends became surrogate members of our family. My mother would feel so comfortable when my friends were around that she showed no hesitation in behaving like their mother. For example, she was very comfortable telling them it was time to go home for supper simply because she was about to prepare our own supper and needed them out of the house. Accordingly, my friends were not the least bit put off by my mother's openness. They simply put on their jackets and went home for their own supper.

In addition, my mother came to know and understand me, my interests, my instincts, my skills, and my ambitions. Following my father's decision to encourage my interest in music, which was also promoted by Grandma Bertha, the responsibility of finding a piano teacher for me fell on my mother's shoulders.

My mother's psychological stability is a bit surprising given the national and global environment in which she was born on February 4, 1920, right at the beginning of a tumultuous decade in the United States. After experiencing the loss of over 100,000 war-related deaths during The Great War (World War I), an additional 600,000 lives were lost near the end of the war from the pandemic which began in the spring of 1918, lasting until 1920. In the end, the loss of 20 million lives globally illustrated the true scope of the disaster that was this pandemic.

The next stress was the passage of the Eighteenth Amendment on January 6, 1919, which created prohibition. Lawlessness exploded during the tumultuous fourteen years of prohibition until its repeal in 1933. "Speakeasies" were underground saloons often run by gangsters, who were supplied with alcohol by "rum runners." The prefix "rum" gradually extended to include all forms of alcohol including whiskey, gin, vodka, and wine. Organized crime in the form of mobsters, Mafia families, and bootleggers ran rampant throughout the country. In spite of prohibition, more alcohol was consumed than at any time prior to the passage of this Eighteenth Amendment.

Coincident with the lawlessness of prohibition was the exuberance of the Roaring Twenties, a decade of fast living and fast women, flapper dresses, and marathon dances. The free-flowing entertainment of the era was coupled with gangster murders and unabashed intoxication. My mother was born into a decade consumed by a search for clarification of the schizophrenic dual personality and identity of the United

States, hovering between fun-loving, carefree happiness on one side and dangerous mobster-dominated lawlessness on the other.

The stock market crash of October 1929 brought an abrupt end to the Roaring Twenties and ushered in the devastating Great Depression of the 1930s. Foreign stresses aggravated those on the home front, chief of which was the rise of Hitler and his antisemitic behavior as well as his quest for supreme power over Europe. These issues and others culminated in World War II, which came to American soil on December 7, 1941, with Japan's unprovoked attack on Pearl Harbor in Hawaii. It is not surprising that my mother's father was very protective of his three daughters during this time of national and global stresses.

Also spanning my mother's early years was the growth of the Ku Klux Klan from 1915 to 1944. The Klan had originated in the South after the Civil War, but beginning in 1915 it had spread to the Midwest states of Indiana, Ohio, and Illinois, where the Klan spread its hatred of not only blacks, but also Jews, Catholics, and immigrants. During this thirty-year span, it claimed as many as six million members.

The Ku Klux Klan was not alone in its religious bigotry. Appearing in print was a publication entitled, *The International Jew: The World's Foremost Problem* in 1921-22, in which it emphasized the following points:

- The immigration problem is Jewish.
- The money problem is Jewish.
- The tie-up of world politics is Jewish.
- The terms of the treaty of peace (WWI) are Jewish.
- The diplomacy of the world is Jewish.
- The moral question in movies and theater is Jewish.
- The mystery of the illicit liquor business is Jewish.

These words were not from Adolph Hitler, and in fact, predated Hitler by ten years. Instead, they were among the writings and publications of Henry Ford. There is no wonder that my father chose to keep secret his Jewish heritage even in this country, far from Germany. Comments such as Ford's were part of rampant antisemitism in the United States during the 1920s. Hitler later embraced these sentiments and put them into brutal action in Germany during the 1930s when his goal was to "purify" the German population. It is mind-boggling to think of both of my parents living, growing, and adapting to these extreme stresses. I feel extremely fortunate to have been guided by these two resilient individuals who were able to navigate and survive the first half of the twentieth century.

The turmoil that my mother went through as she grew into adulthood had the beneficial effect of creating, in her mind, an inspired aspiration to produce a happy marriage followed by a stable and warm family unit, characterized by opportunities for intellectual and artistic growth. I credit her high rating in the personality trait of Conscientiousness.

Interestingly, a new technology in the late 1940s called television helped my mother attain her goals. By 1955, half of American homes had a television set, all black and white. It would be another ten years before color television made significant inroads. This technology became a very important part of our family and provided a much-needed counterweight to all the stresses of the early 20th century. The turmoil of my mother's break with her family, coupled with the uncertainty of life in the United States, which was the result of worry over a potential second world war, led my mother to focus on creating a stable family life for her new husband and their children to be.

With the advent of television, she found models for happy families to emulate in such programs as *Father Knows Best* and *Leave It to Beaver*. These shows depicted stable homes with the father out working, the mother cheerfully managing the home, looking relaxed in a dress and heels in the kitchen, calmly guiding the children through their self-imposed misadventures – all the while awaiting discipline and guidance from the father who returned home after his important work at the office, always wearing a suit and tie.

The episodes demonstrated stability and warmth, always culminating in a happy ending. Then there were the zany, comical, uplifting shows like *I Love Lucy* that helped Americans rise above the dark days of the Depression and the war years. And let's not forget the doctor shows such as *Marcus Welby, MD* and *Dr. Kildaire,* which showed Americans, especially me, that doctors should be pillars of concern and compassion, and not just fountains of knowledge.

Television indeed had an important role to play in the lives of Americans struggling psychologically to adapt to all the emotional stresses of the 1900s. Television programming was designed to highlight the psychological value of distraction, leading to the reduction of our distressed memories of the Great War, the pandemic, Prohibition, the Great Depression, and World War II, as well as encouraging a new focus on life as it should be – warm, connected with peers and family, and optimistic about the future. The television scripts were not intellectually stimulating - they didn't need to be. Instead, the goal was to create emotions that encouraged Americans to forget the past and focus on the present as well as the future.

My parents were both trained in psychiatry, as a physician and a psychiatric nurse. They clearly understood the value of the distraction provided by television, and as a result, we would all gather around the television set in the evening. It enabled us to separate from unfinished homework, medical practice concerns, and household duties. Even though there was work to be done, responsibilities to be fulfilled, and stresses to be resolved, when it was eight o'clock on Monday night and the theme song for *I Love Lucy* was just beginning, it was time to put everything on hold for the next thirty minutes and mix in some laughter.

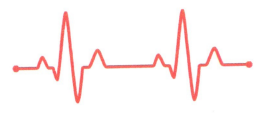

Chapter 10

The Cold War

The 1950s brought even more stress to my mother's efforts to create a stable, worry-free home for her family. While television was lulling the tumultuous events of the first half of the twentieth century into mere memories for many, the fear of communism spreading throughout our country created a foundation for the Cold War between the United States and Russia.

Whether cold or hot, wars always begin with military armament, followed by rhetoric, and then propaganda. The armament phase of the Cold War involved the production and deployment of ballistic missiles equipped with nuclear warheads by both the United States and Russia. What followed next was Russian rhetoric threatening to place ballistic missiles in Cuba, only fifty miles from the United States' coast in 1962. President John Kennedy was able to diffuse this dangerous threat of Russian aggression during what became known as the Cuban Missile Crisis.

However, the 1950s were characterized by strong-felt, smoldering anti-communist propaganda throughout the United States, culminating in the association of communism with the color red. This color reference led to the frequent saying "Better dead than red." The strength of the anti-communism rhetoric reached the United States House of Representatives, where members created the House Unamerican Activities Committee (HUAC). The committee's sole purpose was the identification of individuals suspected of being communist, supporting communism, or spying for communist Russia. Sen. Joseph McCarthy (R-Wisconsin), whose anti-communism ideology (referred to as "McCarthyism") verged on paranoia, amplified and publicized the committee's activities.

In a speech to the Senate, McCarthy asserted that he had a list of communist sympathizers as well as members of a communist spy ring who were scattered among the US State Department, President Truman's administration, and the United States Army. The spread of McCarthy's exaggerated anti-communism rhetoric on top of the prevalent anti-communist fears among the general public led to the destruction of many reputations and careers just by McCarthy's baseless accusations. Individuals seriously affected by McCarthy were included in government, politics, professional occupations, and the entertainment industry. Because of the association of communism with the color red, there was even a halfhearted accusation of communist sympathy leveled at Lucille Ball of *I Love Lucy* simply because her hair was red!

While McCarthy's accusations did accurately identify a few examples of subversive activity in the United States government, most of his suspects were innocent and suffered the loss of promising careers. His influence started to wane in 1954 during the Army-McCarthy hearings in which his overzealous attacks on the loyalty of respected army officers were exposed.

Television played a significant role by telecasting the hearings gavel to gavel, allowing viewers to see for themselves the charlatan that McCarthy was. The Senate subsequently censured McCarthy for his outrageous behavior and he ultimately fell out of the news cycle, passing away in 1957 at age forty-eight of alcoholic cirrhosis of the liver aggravated by his addiction to morphine.

While McCarthy was frightening everyone about communists in our midst, the US military continued to build and deploy ballistic missiles to counter similar efforts in Russia. Fear developed in the United States regarding the vulnerability of large cities such as New York, Chicago, and Los Angeles, representing prime targets for Russian missiles.

Not generally recognized as a potential target, however, was little Bangor, Maine, population 38,000. On the outskirts of our city was Dow Field, a Strategic Air Command (SAC) Air Force base that housed numerous silos containing ballistic missiles with nuclear warheads aimed at Russia. The elimination of Bangor's counterforce to any Russian aggression against the United States was felt to be of high priority in the minds of Russia's military strategists.

My father, always cautious, was so concerned about a nuclear attack on our city that he hired a contractor to build a cinder block bomb shelter in our basement in which we kept bottles of water and canned goods to sustain us in the event of such an attack. The one recommended item to be stored in a bomb shelter which we did not have was a gun for the purpose of preventing others from invading our space in an effort to avoid radiation exposure. There was no way my father or anyone in our family could shoot another person. We would just have to make room. My father proudly displayed in his home office a letter of commendation signed by President Kennedy praising him for his foresight directed at protecting his family in the event of a possible nuclear attack. Fortunately, we never needed to use it.

Chapter 11

The Piano

My mother was a perfect chief operating officer (COO), creating numerous opportunities for me and then activating those opportunities, letting nothing stand in her way. Her perseverance demonstrated a very clear expression of her personality trait of Conscientiousness with its characteristic determination to accomplish whatever she wished.

Such was the case in my music education. Talent without opportunity is talent lost. My mother incorporated this philosophy into every opportunity she found for me to develop my talent, not only on the piano, but also the flute. My music interest and ability derived from the DNA given to me by my father and Grandma Bertha. I am not aware of my grandmother playing any musical instrument, but her interest in and fondness for classical music was legendary and gave me a burgeoning love of melodic, expressive music with its picturesque images. Her interest was transferred to my father's DNA, similarly stimulating

My father and me at the piano in 1980

his interest in impressionist music. He never enjoyed the more modern music of the twentieth century.

His mother, like my mother, provided him with an advanced learning experience on the piano. I say "advanced" deliberately because I came to understand the difficulty of the music of Beethoven he would play while I was in my early years. As an example of his talent, I can still hear him playing Beethoven's *Moonlight Sonata*. The first movement is beautiful and melodic, of intermediate difficulty, given to piano students at an early high school level of experience. The second movement, not often played at this level of experience, is faster and more difficult because of the faster chord progressions. The third and final movement, however, is well beyond high school ability. It is extremely fast with rapid chord progressions and considerably more difficult complexity than the first two movements. Forgive me for going into such detail regarding a single Beethoven composition, but what I'm about to describe regarding my father's playing of the *Moonlight Sonata* speaks volumes about his ability, his training, and his talent.

I never saw my father sit down and practice the piano. I never heard him play scales, octaves, arpeggios, or chord progressions. Yet, on occasion, the mood would strike him and he would sit down at the piano, with no music in front of him and no finger warmup, to play the third movement of the *Moonlight Sonata*. These instances revealed his years of practice of this piece over fifty years ago, with the notes somehow imprinted on his memory. I was impressed as a youngster by his playing of this movement. I knew it sounded difficult and fast, but it was only many years later when I had the time to sit at the piano and attempt to emulate my father that I really understood his level of ability. I managed to make my way through the eight pages of this movement but

Love of the piano certainly is passing through the generations. Here is my grandson, Owen, preparing for his piano recital at age 12.

not as fast as my father could play it. Oh, what memories this difficult music created for me, pushing me to keep working on the piece. "I can do this!"

Unfortunately, seventy-plus-year-old fingers have their limitations. The fact that my father could play this piece by memory in his sixties reflects the quality of his piano teacher and the length of time he spent practicing it, not to mention the numerous exercises required to maintain his level of finger dexterity. Living in a large city like Budapest, Grandma Bertha must have had numerous fine piano teachers to choose from in the development of my father's piano talent. Clearly, he was taught by a great one, as evidenced by his ability to play all three movements of this piece.

Fast forward about twenty-six years, and there I was playing *The Happy Farmer* in my first piano recital at age six. It was not a difficult piece, but I'm sure my father saw a spark of talent. Following our move to Bangor, Maine, he pushed my mother, his chief operating officer, to search for the best opportunity for my talent to develop and thrive. My mother talked to a number of people and discovered that Bangor, small though it was, actually had the Northern Conservatory of Music. This venerable, three-story brick building housed numerous teachers for the piano, violin, woodwinds, voice, and drums/timpani. For the piano, one name rose to the top of the list, Mary Hayes Hayford, an ideal teacher for helping me achieve my father's goal. Her skills gave me an opportunity to flourish in my piano education, similar to what he had received in Budapest.

Ms. Hayford, in fact, had taught a young teenage girl with serious piano talent to a level at which she successfully competed in a piano competition in Europe. In addition, I had the opportunity to hear her play Franz Liszt's *Piano Concerto*, a very difficult piece, accompanied by the Bangor Symphony Orchestra.

I became Ms. Hayford's student at age eight and immediately developed a very strong connection with her as she introduced me to Bach, Mozart, and Beethoven. I was so stimulated by her teaching style and rewarded by her heartfelt compliments that I would get up at six o'clock

I continue to enjoy playing classical piano in our home, partially illuminated by the irony of a leg lamp.

in the morning to practice before school. The amazing part of my early-morning interruption of the family's sleeping pattern was that nobody complained. I wish I could say they were lulled back to sleep by my beautiful melodic playing, but that was not the case as my practice pattern did not include playing a piece from beginning to end. Rather, I would find the difficult parts and then hammer away at them until I achieved a result free of error, a goal which required much repetition. I think my father enjoyed the sounds of my playing. It likely brought back memories of his own playing, perhaps at similar early hours of the day, many years ago. Perhaps my playing actually did lull him back to sleep.

Ms. Hayford would routinely introduce me to a new piano composition by showing me the music. I would typically feel intimidated by the apparent difficulty of the notes because she chose each new piece to advance my playing to a new level. She was such a good teacher; she would sense my apprehension and have me stand at the treble (right) end of the piano while she played the piece for me. I would then fall in love with the music and her melodic playing, prompting me to think to myself, "I can play this; I will do it."

No matter what time of day I chose to work on it, I would become one with the music until it felt like I was playing it as well as I could. Then she would ask me to memorize it, which at ages eight, nine, or ten was not difficult. Remember what I said earlier about children's minds being like sponges? I progressed so rapidly that Ms. Hayford suggested to my parents that I perform a recital in front of their friends, memorizing and playing eight pieces when I was in the fourth grade. My mother made all the arrangements: the guest list, the printed programs, the invitations, the post-recital reception at our home, and the refreshments. I subsequently gave similar recitals in fifth and sixth grades.

At the time, playing the piano well was just something I had learned to do. But for my father, listening to me brought him a source of great pride. Therefore, before each recital, he arranged for me to go to a music store that had a seven-foot grand piano and play all of my pieces while he recorded them on a reel-to-reel tape recorder. He would send the recordings to his brother, Paul, in London. Paul also played the piano as well as the flute. I have all of my tapes and have converted them to CDs, from which I added the music to my iTunes library on my computer. Listening to my music has been extremely interesting as well as nostalgic, revealing my incremental improvement year to year under the guidance of Ms. Hayford. Of special interest to me is the fact that my father recorded his voice announcing the date of the recital and then the name of each composition prior to my playing it. His voice is present on the recording of my first recital. My two subsequent recitals, for reasons that I do not recall, are moderated by my mother's voice. These auditory images are heartwarming and for a few seconds my parents live on.

One of my mother's friends came up to me during a post-recital reception and said she admired my playing so much that she expected one day to hear me playing at Carnegie Hall. While she was correct about the Carnegie Hall part, it was not the piano I played on that venerable stage. Instead, I played the flute when I was in The Harvard Concert Band..

My father's pride in my piano playing was obvious in his support of my interest, especially my focus on music from the classical period, and it was obvious to the friends whom he invited to each of my recitals. His compliments to me, however, were at times quite reserved. I recall an episode on the steps just outside the Conservatory building right after my recital when we stood side-by-side and he said, "Good job, Peter boy. There were a few mistakes, but I don't think anyone noticed." (He always called me "Peter Boy.") Such reserved comments were not at all a problem for me because I was firmly self-motivated, perfecting a new skill from within myself in the form of my desire to be the best I could be.

Ever the cautious person, my father told my mother as his COO on the morning of my third recital to have me stop playing catch with my brother for fear of spraining one of my fingers! As I recall, I thought my father was overreacting and thus continued to play for a few more minutes, revealing my independent personality while also respecting my father's wishes. All of my fingers were fully functional for my recital a few hours later.

As we approach the end of our lives, we have many memories to look back on. In my case, I am fortunate to have these important musical memories combined with the voices of my parents preserved in digital and CD formats for eternity.

Out of all the compositions I played over the years, my all-time favorite is Debussy's *The Sunken Cathedral*, a piano solo which I learned under the guidance of Ms. Hayford and remains my favorite piece to play even now in my seventies. The music reflects the rising and falling of an ornate cathedral, appearing and then disappearing into the sea, with the alternating flow of the tide. As the legend goes, there was a mythical city called "Ys" in which lived a king and his beautiful, but promiscuous daughter. The island on which the city was perched was below sea level. It was protected from flooding by huge, surrounding dikes except for a single gate that would allow the entrance of ships at the proper tide level when the gate would open. After an evening of debauchery with her lover, the daughter stole from her father's cabinet the one and only key to the gate and drunkenly opened it during high tide, consequently flooding and submerging the city and its cathedral. From that moment on, the cathedral would find itself submerged during high tide, only to rise again during low tide.

Debussy's music beautifully reflects the muffled sounds of the submerged cathedral followed by its glorious resurgence with impressive large chords accented by sonorous upper register notes representing the ringing of church bells. Debussy created a masterpiece of music which reflects through impressionist music the imagery of this legend of "Ys". Oh, how my grandmother Bertha would have loved hearing me play this wonderful composition, converting its music into images of the cathedral, rising up from the water, then falling back into the depths of the sea. This piece is rather difficult because of the very large chords sometimes involving nine simultaneous notes, five in the upper register and four in the lower.

Next, I will describe my introduction to the flute, which involved playing only one note at a time. This made my comfort in sight-reading of flute music rather obvious.

Chapter 12

The Flute

When I was thirteen years old, an eighth grader, Ms. Hayford developed a complex neurologic disorder that prevented her from teaching piano. With the loss of her encouragement and compliments, my interest in the piano waned and lay dormant for nineteen years through high school, college, medical school, internship, and cardiology residency. It was not until 1976 at age thirty-two, one year after starting my cardiology practice, that it rose to the surface.

Our new house had a living room with no furniture. What better way to start furnishing a rather large room than buy a baby grand piano? Once in my living room, the beautiful ebony Baldwin piano stoked my dormant enthusiasm for the piano. I started playing my old music, added some popular music, and began extending the level of difficulty of my classical pieces. Now, three pianos later, I am still playing in my seventies, including my all-time favorite Debussy composition, *The Sunken Cathedral*, which sounds even more powerful and exciting on my seven-foot Mason and Hamlin concert piano than it did on my original five-and-a-half-foot Baldwin baby grand piano. I even play my father's favorite *Moonlight Sonata*, including the third movement with all of its challenges, but at a much slower pace than either Beethoven or my father had in mind.

With my musical interest no longer attached to the piano in eighth grade, I told my mother I wanted to play an instrument with other student musicians in the Bangor High School band. A secondary motive was the free tickets for band members to attend and play at all Bangor High School basketball games. In Maine, high school basketball was as popular as football is in Green Bay, Wisconsin. For reasons I cannot recall, I arbitrarily chose the clarinet and asked my mother to go to the music store downtown to rent one for me to try out. However, on the way to the store, she remembered that my uncle Paul in London played the flute. This realization, filtered through my mother's logic, found me an hour later holding a rented flute.

I had no objection to my mother's unrequested change in my plans, primarily because it made perfect sense to me, as most of her recommendations usually did. Piano playing was part of my musical heritage, so why not add the flute? And my father liked the idea, too, further closing the musical loop with his brother.

Once my mother came up with a new plan, she immediately went to work on it. Within a week, she had me sitting next to Herbert Moynihan, an established woodwind instructor at the same Northern Conservatory of Music where I had been taking piano lessons from Ms. Hayford. He was impressed with my musical knowledge derived from the piano, and in no time, I was racing through the beginner's introductory flute workbooks and began working on my tone.

I found the single, one-note-at-a-time flute music amazingly easy to play compared to playing chords on the piano that involved as many as nine notes simultaneously involving both hands. This made sight-reading very simple for me. I could then focus my efforts on learning how to develop the muscles around my lips to create a musical tone that was smooth and sonorous, not rough and breathy. The development of such a skill is a major challenge for any wind instrument player.

My mother's crowning achievement in her efforts to find opportunities for me to further my flute playing occurred unexpectedly in the small Maine coastal town of Hancock. The development of this opportunity actually began years earlier, starting with the internationally famous orchestra conductor, Pierre Monteux. He is best known for his tenure as the conductor of the Boston Symphony Orchestra from 1919-1924, as well as orchestras in Europe, the Netherlands, and other United States cities. He was also distinguished by his refusal in 1916, during World War I, to conduct a New York City orchestra backing up a new ballet called *Till Eulenspiegel*. It turned out this music had been composed by Richard Strauss, who was German. Nazi Germany and its antisemitism were an abomination to Monteux because of his Jewish heritage. He simply could not support the premier of any music originating from within the Nazi state.

Monteux's talents as a conductor are well-preserved in numerous classical albums. Outside of his eloquence as a conductor, he also wanted to create music. He was sufficiently introspective to recognize that he was not a composer, and thus he did the next best thing: he set up a school in Hancock, which happened to be the location of his summer cottage, for young musicians to learn how to play musical instruments and create music. That school had its first class in 1943, and to this day it continues to teach young students how to play various instruments in a beautiful coastal setting.

Monteux's son, Claude, was also a professional musician, conductor, and flutist. Back in those days, there was no home computers for my mother to Google "flute teachers," yet she somehow found out that Monteux was available for flute lessons at his summer cottage in Hancock. I jumped at this opportunity when she told me about it, and a week later I was on my way to Hancock. For the next two summers, in 1961 and 1962, I would leave our cottage on Green Lake and travel the forty-five minutes to spend an hour with M. Monteux, improving my tone and enhancing my appreciation for fine classical flute music. I especially enjoyed playing Mozart's *Flute Concerto in G Major* while M.

The Fergus Trio included Paul on drum, me on flute, and Pat on piano for a Christmas concert in this 1959 photo.

Monteux accompanied me on his upright piano. Instead of practicing the flute all alone at home, it was an inspiring musical experience to hear my solo part magnified by the accompaniment of the piano.

My experience with Monteux, coupled with my tonal improvement that he fostered, propelled me to success in the Maine All-State Band, where I was the first chair flutist for two years. In addition, when I went to Harvard, I had the confidence as a freshman to try out for the university's wind ensemble. Sadly, I was not accepted, but the conductor of the ensemble was also the conductor of the Harvard Concert Band. He was sufficiently impressed by my playing to invite me to become second chair flutist in the concert band, a position I maintained for the four years I spent at Harvard.

My mother was more than the family's chief operating officer in regard to my music opportunities. She was also my agent. Through her numerous contacts in Bangor's music society, she learned the Bangor Symphony Orchestra was looking for a second chair flutist. She let it be known that I was available. I tried out, and at the next rehearsal I was the second chair flutist. And that was not all. She also found out the Bangor City Band needed a flutist and piccolo player (I also played the piccolo), and since the conductor of the band was also the conductor of the Bangor High School band, he took me in without a tryout. He was already familiar with my sight-reading skills and overall playing ability. As an added bonus for the position in the Bangor City Band, I received a small payment for each concert after I joined the Penobscot County Musicians Union as its youngest member.

Beyond music, my mother also created opportunities for me in school and foreign language studies. During several of our after-school conversations while I was in fourth grade, she concluded that I was not being challenged sufficiently in school. She discussed her thoughts with my father and then asked my teacher to give me extra work, usually book reading followed by a book report as well as the assignment of extra math problems. I never felt above anyone in my class or better than anyone else. My parents simply made me feel that I had untapped resources, that I could do better and more than what was being asked of me. I performed my extra work in class quietly without fanfare. There were no ostentatious after-school visits with the teacher to discuss my assignments. My parents were humble, not wanting me to stand out above the others, rather to draw more from within myself. I would hand my extra work to my teacher for her review, after which she would pass her thoughts on to my mother.

My father spoke four languages: English, French, Italian, and Hungarian. When I had mentioned my interest in learning a foreign language, he assigned my mother the responsibility of finding a Spanish teacher for my brother and me. Her search took her to the University of Maine, where she enlisted a professor of the Spanish language, Mr. Gross, who would come to our house every other Tuesday. I progressed sufficiently over the next two years to enter high school Spanish at a third-year level when I was a junior, reading Don Quixote. It helped me to have three years of Latin as an introduction to foreign languages, starting in ninth grade. In addition, I also had three years of French in high school, which enabled me to take a secondary-level French course as a freshman at Harvard.

My mother was also involved in furthering my French language skills.

Toward the end of my sophomore year in high school, she showed me a brochure about a French language summer camp called L'Ecole Arcadie. It took place in Bar Harbor, Maine, in two mansion-style homes that the school rented. The program taught high school students how to speak French by immersing them in French culture for six weeks. I agreed this would be a unique opportunity and entered the program.

Once all of the students settled into their dormitories, French was the only spoken language by us and the teachers. The program lasted six weeks and my fluency improved remarkably. So much so that when I became a Harvard freshman, I was able to enroll in the higher-level French course to further expand my fluency.

L'Ecole Arcadie presented a sophisticated, elegant atmosphere for learning. There were two imposing three-story mansions, surrounded by plush green grass, two tennis courts, and bicycles for exploring the neighborhood – all overlooking the blue ocean waters of Frenchman's Bay bordering Bar Harbor.

Just beyond the two mansions was the Bluenose Ferry dock. Five days a week, the ferry would carry passengers with their cars to Nova Scotia. The passengers could drive around Nova Scotia and then follow the coast line south into Maine. The sound of the ferry horn announcing its morning departure at 7 am was a pleasant reminder that breakfast would soon be ready. The camp's administrator, Monsieur Gott, was responsible for the many teachers and fifty-plus students.

The two mansions served as dorms, the girls in the more sophisticated stucco construction building, the boys in a wood frame, more casual ranch-style construction. I was never aware of any cohabitation going on, but that type of activity was of no interest to me because I had a steady girlfriend, Kathy, back home who was spending the summer working as a telephone operator. In any case, the girls at L'Ecole Arcadie knew that I was off-limits. The mail room was in the girls' dorm, and it was therefore obvious that I was receiving daily letters from someone who had feminine penmanship. They were also aware of my frequent outgoing posts to the person on the return address of these letters. Yes, I was not only off-limits, but also already taken!

My father was well aware of my mother's activities seeking opportunities for me to grow and develop so I could confront multiple challenges. Furthermore, he knew that if it were not for her actions, there would never have been flute music in our home or names like Claude Monteux, Pierre Monteux, Mary Hayes Hayford, or L'Ecole Arcadie. He was always in perfect agreement with her judgments except for one issue: my choice of college. I vividly remember the occasion that my father chose to bring up this disagreement.

All of our family discussions routinely occurred around the dinner table, but on this occasion he wanted to talk with me in private, specifically about my choice of college when I was a junior in high school. It was in the spring and he came outside to talk with me when I was kneeling in the backyard clipping weeds along our home's concrete foundation. I do not recall my father ever venturing into the backyard, especially if it meant leaving the house by the front door and walking around the side of the house. It simply never happened!

I therefore knew something important was up; something was on his mind that he did not want to discuss in front of my mother. What was on his mind concerned the "big picture" about my future, a decision worthy of the chief executive officer who had an opinion and recommendation at odds with my mother, his chief operating officer. He was always acutely aware of the feelings of others and did not want to hurt my mother's feelings by what he wanted to say to me. My mother had been suggesting that I apply to a small, but respected men's school, Hamilton College, which was only fifty-two miles from her hometown of Binghamton, New York.

My father, however, had bigger aspirations for me, having watched me grow, successfully conquer the piano and flute, get good grades in the classroom, and do very well in three foreign languages. He, therefore, saw me as a very good candidate for an Ivy League school with an international reputation such as Harvard. He also recognized the importance of a college education as a first step in my path through graduate school, which he hoped would be medical school, internship, residency, and specialty fellowship. He also was well aware of my personality trait of conscientiousness with its focus on determination and goal-motivation.

Our private discussion in the backyard, clippers in hand, had my father's desired effect. I never applied to Hamilton College, but I did apply to and was accepted by both Harvard and Princeton. My father knew me well and so did Harvard, which presented me with The Harvard Book Award, given to the highest-ranking high school junior boy. (Girls from Radcliffe shared classes with Harvard students, but the administrations of the two schools were separate until 1999, when Harvard and Radcliffe officially merged.)

I'm sure my father explained our conversation in the backyard to my mother in a most thoughtful way so as not to offend her. My "safe school" for college applications was Amherst, but interestingly enough, I was only wait-listed! My parents' actions, with their complementary focuses as CEO and COO had immense implications for my life. They helped me develop a foundation for the self-confidence required for future independent decision-making to benefit myself, my family, and my patients.

Arising from their distinct personality traits were guidelines that filtered down to my advantage. My mother's guiding principle was: "Talent without opportunity is talent lost." My father's guiding principle was: "A conscientious personality without optimum opportunities is a personality unfulfilled."

One could not ask for a more complementary parent pair to supervise, encourage, and guide me through my early years. My mother gave me every opportunity to flower, while my father helped me blossom into a confident young man ready to seek his own opportunities.

Chapter 13

Rita's Devotion

My mother doted on my father, her love pouring forth in everything she did for him. She supported him in his practice, functioning as his first office nurse. She tended to his every personal need when it came to his laundry, his ironing, his home decorating, and his favorite foods (stuffed green pepper and rare roast beef). He gave her full responsibility for the care of the house, including her choice of a cleaning lady every two weeks.

When she would hear his car enter the driveway, she would make his favorite – and only – cocktail, Four Roses whiskey with ginger ale. She would place his mail on the dining room table next to his drink, and there would be a separate pile for Grandma Bertha's mail. Supper was a family affair. It was the one opportunity for parents and children to share thoughts, ideas, and activities of the closing day. We never sat down to eat until my father was home and ready to eat with us: Mother's Rule.

With two women loving and caring for the same man (my mother and Grandma Bertha), there were unavoidable conflicts, especially when they all shared the same determination, assertiveness, and compassion characteristics of their high scores in the personality traits of extroversion, openness, agreeableness, and conscientiousness. The relationship between my grandmother, mother, and father – all strong-willed but sensitive, empathetic individuals – deserves further analysis because of the number of interacting dynamics. For example, these three individuals had overlapping relationships which they attempted to coalesce within a very complicated setting.

There was my Grandmother Bertha, the mother of my father, André, and mother-in-law of my mother, Rita. Meanwhile, Rita was the wife of André and daughter-in-law of Bertha. Simultaneously, André was the son of Bertha and husband of Rita. Each relationship had dual qualities, double allegiances, and different expectations. Hovering above all of these complexities was André's role as a referee, whose responsibility was to keep both of the women happy who loved him so dearly. Complicated? Yes. Impossible? No. My father, remember, was a psychiatrist, an expert in managing emotions.

His first assessment of this combination of his mother and wife living in the same house prompted only one conclusion: it was unsustainable. As much as his mother had done to support him in his European travels while he progressed through his education, her job was done. She had had completed her self-imposed task, which was to help him develop his interest in medicine. Any further support for the advancement in his practice of psychiatry was now his wife's responsibility.

The order of influence of these two women was now reversed, with Rita now number one and Bertha number two. This was not an easy adjustment for these two women. My father focused his attention on the best way to amicably separate Bertha from Rita. He started by convincing Bertha that she would be happier in her own apartment and suggested something that he himself would have loved to do, namely move to Florida. As dedicated as he was to his psychiatry practice, he found it difficult to acclimate to the cold weather of Maine and wished that he could move his practice to Florida. Thus, his recommendation that his mother rent an apartment in Florida seemed very desirable to him, and he projected that desire onto his mother.

It took a couple of years and multiple trips to Florida, but he ultimately found a nice apartment for his mother in St. Petersburg. However, as desirable as Florida was for him, he failed to recognize that the beauty of the palm trees and the warmth of the weather fell far short of compensating for Bertha's separation from her beloved son. As a result, the Florida experiment lasted less than two years before Bertha made a surprise return to our home. I was happy to have her back, as were my brother and sister. My mother, predictably, was not. My father was ambivalent, knowing the challenges that lay ahead, but he still wanted his mother to be happy and comfortable.

The next step, of course, was finding an apartment for Bertha in Bangor. My mother, as chief operating officer, took on that responsibility, and after a few months she found an apartment above a dental office in an established home less than a mile away. In the meantime, Bertha generally hibernated upstairs in her bedroom reading books (sometimes books that I was reading!) and *The New York Times*. She would come downstairs after my father arrived and interact with all of us. This separation successfully avoided any direct conflict with my mother.

Before Bertha moved to Florida, there was a significant combination of events that involved a disagreement between the three adults over the Hungarian language being spoken in our home. It was a disagreement that had an unintended consequence. I was only a young teenager and have no recollection of the nature of the argument that took place in our dining room that day. (Remember, it was in a language I did not speak or understand.) No voices were raised, and all I remember was that it ended with Bertha saying something to André in Hungarian and he responded. My mother was never afraid of confrontation and assumed that the Hungarian comments were criticisms of her. She reacted by facing off to Bertha and André, ordaining that never again would Hungarian be spoken in our home.

You might think: "Well, all right. Case closed; no more Hungarian language. Mama got what Mama wanted." But no. The unintended consequence began, oddly enough, in the forest just outside Budapest. It was 1956 and the Hungarian government was getting too cozy with Russia. The rank-and-file Hungarian population was very much against any close association with Russia, which led to the Hungarian uprising and the subsequent invasion of Hungary by Russia in that year. At that time, my father's cousin, Gusti, his wife, Magda, and their six-year-old son, Peter, were living successful lives in Budapest. As the Russian tanks rolled into Budapest, however, they fled their home and ran through the woods outside Budapest, carrying a few of their belongings along with them. They made their way slowly into Austria, where they ultimately obtained passports, traveled to New York City, and contacted my father.

The Hungarian uprising was big international news, with prominent exposure on network television. A more interesting story than the political conflict was the human struggle illustrated by the escape of my father's relatives from Hungary to the United States, especially the fact that it was occurring during the Cold War with Russia. Their personal struggle and its associated danger became more poignant when reporters learned that Gusti and his family had a Hungarian relative in America, namely a psychiatrist named Andrew Fergus, MD, in Bangor, Maine.

This Hungarian family's struggle became such a hot story that one of the national news networks arranged to bring Gusti and his family into the New York City television studio to speak live to my father by telephone. My father's responsibility was to converse with Gusti in Hungarian and then translate what he said to the television audience. This is where the unintended consequence of my mother's prohibition of the Hungarian language in our home came into play. After the program was over, I recall my father telling my mother that the conversation in Hungarian was difficult for him because his fluency in the Hungarian language had deteriorated and he had forgotten the English translation for some of the words that Gusti was saying. This handicap could be traced back to my mother's prohibition of Hungarian in our home

My father (far right) escorts his mother, Bertha, during my brother Paul's wedding in 1968. On the left are my mother and my father's Hungarian cousin, Gusti.

several years earlier. Nothing further was said, and I really doubt my mother inferred his comment as any reflection of the language prohibition that she had, in fact, ordained in the past. In any case, it never came up in front of me.

I had an opportunity to meet Gusti and his family in 1966 when they came to Kathy's and my wedding. Gusti had become a successful businessman in New York City over the preceding ten years, Magda had opened her practice as a CPA accountant, and Peter would go on to be accepted at Harvard.

The events originating from a simple family argument demonstrate how very strong my mother's drive was to maintain her well-earned closeness to her husband in the face of his most influential mother.

My parents at the American Medical Association's annual banquet, c. 1966

She also displayed a determined effort to protect her husband after he had experienced an adverse decision from the medical staff at Eastern Maine Medical Center. The sequence of events went as follows:

My mother's personality traits of extroversion and conscientiousness were on full display shortly after our arrival in Bangor in 1952. My father was just starting his practice in psychiatry and joined the Penobscot County Medical Society in order to be part of the medical community and meet family practice doctors who could be sources of referrals. At the same time, my mother joined the Women's Medical Society Auxiliary. Even though my father was the only psychiatrist north of Portland, his application for staff privileges at this major hospital in Bangor was denied. The reason was never clear, but my father believed it was due to the unfamiliarity of the medical community with his focus on a new form of psychiatric treatment for severe depression and schizophrenia called electroconvulsive therapy, or ECT. This new form of therapy was met with suspicion and uncertainty by the doctors of Bangor, who did not understand its rationale, efficacy, or safety.

Bear in mind, Bangor was a small provincial medical community where the doctors were unaware of my father's extensive experience with ECT at the VA Hospital in Canandaigua, New York, for two years. Nor were they aware of the paper on ECT that he had written and was published in the *Journal of the American Psychiatric Association* in December 1952. I actually found it in the archives of the library in the University of Rochester School of Medicine when I was a medical student there.

There was also suspicion arising from the fact that my father was a foreigner and foreign-trained, even though he had passed the ECFMG exam required of all foreign medical graduates who wish to practice medicine in this country. He was fully qualified to practice medicine, a privilege that was further enhanced by his internship and residency in psychiatry performed in Brooklyn, Binghamton, and Canandaigua — all in New York State.

My mother did not take lightly to this affront to my father's qualifications and took matters into her own hands. Her personality trait of extroversion enabled her to easily make friendships with other women within the Medical Society Auxiliary. Then, the determination arising from her conscientiousness resulted in her election to none other than the presidency of the auxiliary. So take that you doubting Thomases! Being a psychiatric nurse, she understood through actual experience how ECT works and how effective it was in the treatment of severe depression and schizophrenia. She was able to educate the doctors' wives, who could then educate their husbands.

Meanwhile, my father was demonstrating in real time the effectiveness of ECT with dramatic improvement in the mental health of patients suffering from these life-changing mental diseases. As a result, he was granted consulting privileges at the hospital after a year or two, but not ECT privileges. This denial, however, was not a problem because he was able to do all the ECT required for his patients' care at Utterbach Private Hospital, to which he added outpatient procedures in his office with my mother functioning as his nurse. Teamwork! My mother was simply there when needed, whether standing up for his credentials or assisting him in the performance of his unique therapy.

I cannot let this chapter close without revealing a lighter side of my mother's personality. As strong a force as she was in so many aspects, she did have a tendency to look for short cuts. These short cuts had a very practical origin: why waste energy on activities that can be done more simply without sacrificing quality?

The first example was her decision to elope, thereby avoiding conflict with her own father and sparing my father the embarrassment of being personally snubbed, not to mention avoiding the very impractical expense of a reception party. The second example was a short cut she discovered in the preparation of my father's favorite dessert, hazelnut cake. Bertha's recipe called for the whites of a dozen eggs, no yokes. My mother followed this rather tedious portion of the recipe for several years. But along the way, she discovered a packet of a dozen dried egg whites while preparing a boxed angel food cake. She was able to eliminate the tedium of cracking twelve eggs without changing the quality of the cake, and my father was no worse for this adjustment. Problem solved; everybody happy.

Her third and most controversial short cut involved what I call the "irony of ironing." For years, just like her mother-in-law, she always ironed my father's shirts. That is, until she took note of the fact that my father never took off his suit coat when he was in the office seeing patients. The back of his shirt was never revealed, so why spend the time smoothing out those wrinkles? Starting from that epiphany, she only ironed the front of his shirts because, after all, who was ever going to see the back? My wife, whose approach to anything was perfection and completeness, was appalled, but smart enough never to confront my mother over it.

In any case, my father was happy with his shirts; my mother saved electricity and personal energy; and, importantly, my mother's personal short cut, when revealed, always received a good laugh! These shortcuts were a reflection of my mother's conscientiousness, with her determination to get a job done in whatever way was required.

Another example occurred in an emergent situation. My father had just arrived home in Canandaigua and parked our 1950's Dodge sedan in the driveway, which had a downward slope. He had forgotten to set the parking brake, and the car began rolling down the hill toward the garage. My mother had come out to greet him, and fortunately was still standing near the car. She quickly opened the door, jumped in, and stepped on the brake to prevent the car from rupturing the garage door. I was only six years old and still have a vivid memory of my mother's quick-thinking, courageous action to save the car and the garage. My father was impressed, too.

Determined, bold, fearless. That was my mother.

Chapter 14

"Bandi"

My father, André Forgacs (Hungarian nickname: Bandi), was blessed with a keen mind, a calm and comforting personality, and a strong drive to accomplish goals despite the presence of various obstacles. If these qualities sound familiar, just think "Mother Bertha." She navigated both of her sons through three European countries and three different universities and colleges of medicine. Each of these changes involved substantial risk taking, especially in a person as small and unimposing as my grandmother was at four feet, eight inches.

My father showed the same willingness to confront risk in the presence of new opportunities in spite of his small frame of five feet, four inches and understated demeanor. There was much genetic material passed from Bertha's generation to André's and then on to me. The following points illustrate the importance of these genetics.

I was present when my father made the decision to move our family to a state in which he had never set foot and probably had never heard of during his time in Europe. I was present when he made the trip to Minot, North Dakota, where he requested a $5,000 loan ($50,000 in 2024 dollars) to get his practice started. I was present when he accepted the opportunity to run the psychiatry department at a small private hospital in Bangor. I was present when he made his plans to introduce electroconvulsive therapy (ECT) to his patients while educating his referring doctors about the value of this new technology.

Being present, however, is a far cry from understanding the risks associated with the decisions being discussed. I was only eight years old. What did I know about risk? My world was stable, comfortable, warm, and loving. Actions led to predictable reactions. I had no comprehension of the momentous risks attendant upon my father's proposal to create the psychiatry practice of his dreams, which also included the personal and professional participation of my mother as well as the move of his entire family to parts unknown. I was only a naïve, unknowing observer. Therefore, my subsequent comfort with risk taking in my own professional life was not the result of observation of my father's risk taking.

Instead, my adult comfort with risk taking was genetically determined. It started with Grandma Bertha, passed through my father, André, and then on to me when I became faced with new opportunities. For now, I would like to analyze the steps my father took to prepare for his confrontation with the risks that he knew he would be facing in his effort to create the ideal form of care for patients with mental illness. It was a level of care completely unknown in a vast area of Maine.

My father was very eager to leave Europe and come to the United States. Europe was in turmoil because of so many countries packed together with arguments over ethnicity, complicated by border conflicts. There was also the depression created by the draconian elements of the Treaty of Versailles, which terminated the Great War. In addition, there was the unrest created by the brutality of Adolf Hitler as well as the explosion of previously simmering antisemitism. My father was also stymied in his educational requirements because of Hungary's relationship with Nazi Germany and the subsequent restrictions on educational opportunities in his native Budapest. He fortunately had the extraordinary love and support of his mother, who guided him through the risk of changing countries, changing living quarters, and changing educational opportunities. These factors made his learning journey quite difficult, not to mention the need to become fluent in three different languages: Italian, French, and English.

Once he completed his studies, he took the risk of following his dream of moving to the United States. He boarded the HMS Queen Mary (I believe) and arrived in New York City in 1935 with no support system and no prearranged living arrangements. He then passed the Educational Commission for Foreign Medical Graduates (ECFMG) exam, enabling him to become an intern at a hospital in Brooklyn, New York. Mother Bertha joined him in 1939, following which he became a resident in psychiatry at Binghamton State Hospital. That is where he met my mother and took on the risk of keeping two women happy, both of whom loved him dearly and would go to the ends of the earth to support him.

He studied American history during this period and became a naturalized United States citizen, a certificate of which he proudly displayed in his apartment. After his initial residency experience at the State Hospital in Binghamton, he moved to Canandaigua, New York, where he continued his psychiatric education at the VA Hospital. He focused on ECT, at the time a new psychiatric treatment for schizophrenia and severe depression. The basis for ECT was the observation that patients who experienced spontaneous seizures from epilepsy oftentimes awoke with significant improvement in their depressive or schizophrenic symptoms. This observation led to the development of electrical machines that could artificially create seizure activity in the brain by affecting the brainwave pattern.

In order to prevent the usual limb flailing that occurs during natural seizures, a medication called succinylcholine created temporary muscle paralysis. One of the muscles affected by this medication, however, was

My father and I were all smiles on my wedding day in 1966.

the diaphragm, which controls breathing. Thus, respiratory support had to be provided by an ambu bag, which commonly is used today for ventilatory support during a cardiac arrest. Succinylcholine paralyzed only skeletal muscle and not cardiac muscle. Therefore, patients maintained normal blood pressures and heart rates during the ECT procedure. The effects of interrupted breathing would last only about ten minutes, following which all muscle activity, including the diaphragm, returned to normal.

My father allowed me to observe an ECT procedure in his office on one occasion, and I found it quite alarming to witness a patient not breathing on their own. For my father and his nurse, however, it was an everyday procedure. He had become an expert in this procedure through his experience at the Canandaigua VA hospital, and he wrote a paper that was published in the *American Journal of Psychiatry* in December 1952. Getting a scientific paper published in a national specialty journal is a major accomplishment, specially originating from a nonacademic institution such as the VA hospital in little Canandaigua, New York. Its acceptance for publication is a reflection of the importance of my father's research in ECT, a new approach to resolving previously untreatable schizophrenia and severe depression.

My father did not want to stay in a government-supported hospital forever. He was determined to establish a private practice of psychiatry where he could not only apply his expertise in ECT, but also his knowledge of the new psychiatric medications. The FDA had only recently approved Elavil and Thorazine for the treatment of severe depression and schizophrenia, respectively. But where to go?

In spite of his dislike of cold weather, he found, through classified sections of psychiatric journals, a perfect opportunity in many respects. He did his research and found that there were no psychiatrists north of Portland in Maine. Bear in mind that Portland is only fifty miles inside the southern state line. In between Portland and the northernmost city in Maine (Madawaska) at the Canadian border was a distance of 333 miles. Meanwhile, Bangor is 130 miles north of Portland and 215 miles south of Madawaska, regions with no psychiatrists and no ECT. This geography presented an obvious opportunity for my father to locate his practice in a wide-open territory.

Another reason for choosing Bangor for his practice was the availability of a small private hospital that had just lost its only physician. Such small hospitals were not uncommon back in those days and were frequently dependent on a single medical doctor. This one was named after its owner, Mr. Utterbach, who happened to be a blazing Boston Red Sox fan. He carried a little transistor radio everywhere he went when the Red Sox were playing. My father knew nothing about baseball and had never even heard of the Red Sox until he took my brother and me to a game. I tried unsuccessfully to explain the game and the star players (Mickey Mantle, Roger Maris, and Ted Williams) before I became, I admit, somewhat frustrated.

My father's opportunity to convert this private hospital into a psychiatric hospital, with provisions for the application of ECT therapy and using new medications in the treatment of seriously ill patients, seemed like a gift from heaven. In his mind, I'm sure he felt it was almost too good of an opportunity to be true. But it WAS true, and only a few months later, after getting a loan from his Hungarian friend, Tiberius Donat — who had previously set up a very successful medical practice in Minot, North Dakota — my brother, my grandmother, my father, and myself were in our old maroon Dodge sedan on the highway to Bangor.

My mother and sister, Patricia, flew to Bangor a couple of weeks later, landing in the city's small airport that was new to the flying public. Flying was considered risky in those days, and like many airports, there was a machine along the wall that dispensed insurance policies just in case a flying "mishap" occurred. This outpost-style airport subsequently became a big deal when the air force moved in and added missile silos in the process of becoming a Strategic Air Command base to protect all of us during the Cold War with Russia.

My father was very serious about the dangers of a nuclear attack by Russia on our missiles. He therefore built the first bomb shelter in the region in our basement. He rented an office on State Street, one of the main thoroughfares of downtown Bangor, right across the street from a large grocery store. Even today, there is considerable embarrassment among some patients when seeing a psychiatrist, but it was quite exaggerated back in the 1950s, to the point that patients would often hide their visit with my father by parking their cars in the grocery store lot.

The opportunities afforded him were immense, but also immense were the risks, not to mention the debt acquired to get his practice going. He had no support system among the medical community other than a few physicians to whom he was introduced by the Utterbachs. He needed a secretary, who turned out to be quite challenging because of her typing skills – or lack thereof. My mother was his registered nurse in the beginning. He later found a highly qualified, extremely effective nurse who assisted him with patient care and ECT treatments, both in the office and in the hospital.

My father's practice flourished rapidly; so rapidly, in fact, that after the first year he was able to repay in full the loan he had received from Dr. Donat. There were a number of reasons for his rapid success. The most important was his personality trait of agreeableness. His patients, therefore, saw him as warm, sensitive, charming, and concerned; everything a patient could possibly want in a physician of any specialty, especially one focused on mental health. A second contributor to his rapid success was the effectiveness of his scientific approach to psychiatry with new medications, state-of-the-art ECT therapy, and an ability to listen with concern to his patients' conflicts. Thirdly, he projected a surrogate image of Sigmund Freud, who was well-known to the average person during the 1950s and 1960s. Freud was an Austrian neurologist. My father was from Hungary, adjacent to Austria. They both spoke English with similar Slavic accents. My father's Hungarian accent, as well as his foreign origin, therefore created a distinct link to this famous physician and gave him immediate respect and trust among patients.

Although he conjured up images of the best-known psychiatrist of that era, it is doubtful that the average person in Maine knew anything about Freud's theories other than a "Freudian slip," which is a reference to the substitution of an unexpected word for the anticipated one, revealing in the process a subconscious conflict.

Freud's theory of human psychology was based on the fact that the human psyche is divided into three parts: the ego, the id, and the superego. The ego represents reality, with the world and the personalities within it taken at face value. The id portion of our psyche, according to Freud, harbors our basic subconscious instincts, separate from reality and oftentimes reflecting sexual conflicts originating during our childhood years. Meanwhile, the superego is our conscience, helping us distinguish between right and wrong. Conflicts between our instincts (id) and conscience (superego) are settled by the ego, which functions as a referee. Unresolved conflicts with which the ego is struggling are resolved by psychiatrists trained in a special type of therapy called psychoanalysis, popularized in movies and on television as a patient lying languidly on a couch as the doctor encourages them to revisit childhood conflicts. In addition, dreams were analyzed for hints of unresolved conflicts and unfulfilled wishes, according to Freudian theory.

When I was in college, I found Freudian theory quite interesting and fun to think about, as well as a great discussion point for conversations with my roommates. My father did not consider himself a Freudian psychiatrist, however, and did not engage in psychoanalysis. Instead, he practiced psychotherapy, which simply involves listening to patients describe their current interpersonal conflicts and then helping them devise ways to resolve them. This is now called behavioral therapy.

I have no recollection of any conversations with my father regarding Freudian theory or even the terms ego, id, and superego. My father was board certified in neurology as well as psychiatry, and very much enjoyed the scientific explanation of neurologic events rather than Freudian theories. He focused on brain anatomy, coupled with his knowledge of nerve distribution, to explain neurologic events such as the sequelae of strokes. His rapid success was accomplished without the help of social media which would not be developed until many decades later. Instead, his reputation rapidly expanded as the result of patients' successful experiences with his therapy, and their subsequent compliments expressed to others by word of mouth.

While my father's foreign accent was an advantage for attracting patients, it was a disadvantage for matriculating into Bangor's general medical community. The reason was very simple: jealousy. His popularity made him a potent competitor against the general practitioners in Bangor who felt that they were already practicing psychiatry by way of general psychology. The practice of general medicine frequently involves attention to psychological issues to help patients deal with stress-related issues such as hypertension, anxiety, and depression. Without understanding my father's new scientific approach to mental illness, they considered his presence in Bangor, in a word, unnecessary.

This jealousy did not pervade the entire general medical community, but there were several individual physicians whom I could easily infer as unlikely referral sources just by listening to dinnertime conversations with my mother. Nevertheless, it made no matter because my father was determined to introduce a new approach to psychiatric disease management involving the new medications of Elavil and Thorazine, as well as the practice of electroconvulsive therapy. His focus on this scientific method left no room for Freudian psychoanalytic therapy. It helped him ultimately stand out in the minds of many Bangor physicians as a psychiatrist who indeed practiced his craft in a much different manner than what was being practiced routinely in medical offices.

The rapid expansion of his patient load spoke volumes regarding his success with this advanced form of treatment for mental illness, amplified by his unique style of warmth, empathy, and intelligence. His unintended comparison with Freud may have brought patients into his office, but it was his inimitable style that led them to return.

Chapter 15

Everyday Life
Terms of Endearment

Since the twelfth century, our culture has recognized that addressing a loved one requires a special form of salutation. "Hey you" is neither appropriate nor desirable. Therefore, our language developed a form of address which embodies closeness and caring, if not true love.

The original forms of endearment were "honey" and "sweetheart." The operative emotion of these terms refers to sweetness, meaning pleasing to the senses, including the mind, as well as the feelings arising from the Old English word "swette." During our caveman evolution, sweetness in food became desirable for the provision of sugar needed as fuel for our muscles, which would be called upon when fighting or fleeing from danger. So, sweetness became something not only desirable, but also necessary for our reproductive survival. It is obvious how these early terms of sweetness found their way to a loved one, someone necessary for our happiness, longevity, and especially our reproductive capacity. These sweet references then expanded to terms reflecting anyone who is desirable, with words like "doll" and "darling."

While this discussion of terms of endearment makes perfect sense, we come to a bit of a roadblock when we arrive at my father's word choice for endearment, i.e. "toots." The derivation of this term appears to arise from the word "tootsie" used to refer to a baby's little foot. The connection, therefore, must have been: "Who cannot be emotionally charged by the cute little foot of a baby, his tootsie?" Remember my father was not a native English speaker and apparently felt the word "toots" was just plain cute. In addition, very likely the cuteness of the words "toots" and "tootsie" were amplified by a popular song of the 1920s with the lyrics: "Toot, toot, tootsie goodbye. Toot, toot, tootsie don't cry. Kiss me, tootsie and then do it all over again."

These words and their accompanying musical ditty certainly sound-

Our father always wore a tie and suspenders, even at the beach. This is me in my chubby phase (left), Pat and Paul, c. 1958.

A Life Worth Living

We were very involved with Cub Scouts as kids. That's me on the far left, my brother Paul is second from right in the glasses, and our mother (back right) was one of the den mothers. I was about ten years old, which would make this photo c. 1954.

ed cute and attractive, but when I give you a few more lines of the above verse, you will see the two faces of the Roaring Twenties: the unabashed, freewheeling, fun-loving face, balanced against the lawless, gangster-driven violence of that period. For example, take the line that comes right after: "Kiss me tootsie and then do it all over again." Specifically: "And if you don't get a letter from me, you'll know I'm in jail."

Then consider these subsequent lines imploring his girlfriend not to cry: "That little choo-choo train that takes me away, Away from you, no words can tell how sad it makes me." The train is taking him away from his girlfriend as he is being transferred to jail for bootlegging whiskey and rum, and that is the reason he is going to be so sad. In actual fact, an excessive amount of alcohol was consumed during the thirteen prohibition years that powered the fun-loving activity of the Roaring Twenties.

The fun of alcohol-powered playfulness as provided by bootleggers and speakeasies came at a cost of incarceration, as reflected in this

(From left) My brother Paul, his wife Nancy, Kathy and I were together on the Maine coast for lunch in 2023.

tune. It may seem completely incongruous for my father, a serious lover of Italian opera, to walk into our home singing *Toot, Toot, Tootsie*. However, it makes perfect sense when one realizes this tune is distinctly American and my father loved being a United States citizen. In fact, he felt more at home singing an American ditty like *Toot, Toot, Tootsie* than a verse from an Italian aria.

In any case, my father always called my mother Toots. He never called her Rita unless he was referring to her in a conversation with friends. My grandmother and mother called my father Bandi, a Hungarian nickname for André, which in turn was Hungarian for Andrew. My father's friends always called him André, not Andrew, and never Andy. Both my father and mother called Grandma Bertha "Anya," the Hungarian word for mother. Meanwhile, my father referred to me as Peter Boy and my brother as Paul Boy. He referred to my sister, Patricia, as Babe unless he was speaking of her to other people, when he would refer to her as Patsy.

Home Layout

My brother and I shared one of two bedrooms upstairs in our new and only home in Bangor, while my sister and grandmother shared the second one. In the short hallway between the two bedrooms and at the top of the stairway was a closet with a pocket door. There were six people living in our 2,000-square-foot home with only one bathroom, which was situated on the first floor adjacent to my parents' bedroom. Bathroom sharing became so complex that my father hired a carpenter

My sister, Pat VanLeuven, and her husband, Bill

to convert the upstairs closet into a bathroom with a sink and a toilet very soon after we moved in. This additional bathroom also served as my grandmother's private domain for her prolonged visits to the toilet while she read *The New York Times*. This made that bathroom off limits to everyone else for two hours or more. You can imagine my mother's frustration during the time that we had only one bathroom in the house, with that single bathroom reserved by her mother-in-law for two hours.

Completing our home's upstairs layout, the attic ultimately was converted to an additional bedroom so that my brother and I did not have to share a room. Downstairs, besides the usual living room, dining room, mudroom, and kitchen were a piano room and a study. While the use of the piano room is obvious, the study was multifunctional. My father would use it for his office chart dictations, which he did every Sunday, and I frequently used it on weekday afternoons as a quiet study hall. More importantly, this room still carries memories for me as the location of our Spanish lessons with the professor from the University of Maine, and more personally, it was where my father enlightened me about the "birds and the bees," as well as my Jewish heritage during my teenage years.

Paul and Pat's Music Education

My mother was a strong supporter of my interest and ability in the piano and flute. She also wanted to support my brother in music, and intuitively, she chose the drums for him. She also enrolled Paul in tap dancing classes. This rather unique combination of activities suggests that my mother felt Paul had an overabundance of energy and was in desperate need of an outlet. Ultimately, however, Paul's drum teacher steered him into the creation of melodic music through lessons on the marimba, at which he became quite proficient.

Meanwhile, my sister, Pat, focused on the piano. When this instrument led to boredom, she followed in my footsteps and studied the flute, also making it to the Maine Allstate Band and being compared favorably to me.

Manners

My mother's influence extended well beyond the arts. She enrolled my brother and me in ballroom dancing class, where we learned much more than how to do the waltz and the foxtrot. More importantly, we learned about social graces: how to meet a stranger and give a firm handshake, and how to introduce a friend to an adult or even to another friend. Additionally, my mother personally made sure that I knew the most important social grace, which is modesty.

This particular educational experience required only one session between my mother and me. Innocently enough, it occurred spontaneously at the dining room table. Both my brother and I had recently received nice watches, but considerably different in their shape. I was bragging about the unusual triangular shape of my watch versus Paul's more traditional round shape. My mother listened quietly to this spirited conversation. Later, when she caught me alone, she pointed out that Paul looked up to me as his older brother, and therefore, it was improper and just plain wrong for me to put him down. I never bragged to anyone ever again about one of my possessions. Her words were logical and powerful.

The evening dinner table was also a very important source of education for all three of the Fergus children. Table manners were of prime importance. "Keep your elbows off the table;" "Do not slurp your milk;" "Say 'please' when asking for the butter to be passed;" "Don't start eating until everyone has his food in front of him;" "Don't talk with your mouth full," and so on. Discussions were encouraged; arguments were not.

A portion of manners is thoughtfulness, which my mother had to the extreme. She came to give Kathy a helping hand just after our first born, Scott, arrived. Since my father always had a woman at home, from Grandma Bertha to my mother, he had no reason to engage in any culinary skills. So in preparation for her week-long absence, she made his favorite sandwich: salami and cheese on dark rye. She prepared twenty-one of them, lovingly placed in the refrigerator, one for lunch and two for dinner!

We still joke about this act of thoughtfulness, because it was so typical of my mother's caring and concern for my father combined with her focus on shortcuts. What happened to frozen hamburgers and frozen casseroles? Twenty-one sandwiches should be enough!

Grammar

We also focused on proper grammar of the English language, especially in regard to the proper use of pronouns and verbs. Him/her are object pronouns and should never be used as the object of a verb. For example, "Him and I went to the fair." (No no!) We were also careful about verbs. For example, "I seen a bear yesterday." (No no!).

We all took Latin for three years in high school. As a result, were very familiar with verb conjugation. For my father, English was a second or perhaps third language after Hungarian. As a result, he thoroughly studied English grammar. I never heard him make a grammatical mistake.

As our three boys were growing up, Kathy and I continued to emphasize the educational value of dinner time conversations, with everyone waiting to sit down at the table only after I arrived home from the office, when we could all sit down together and start sharing experiences.

Chapter 16

Religion, Politics, and Hugs

Religion

Religion was an important topic of discussion between my parents. However, despite the diversity of their upbringing, there was really no conflict. My mother had a very strong Catholic upbringing courtesy of her religious parents. Meanwhile, in spite of my father's Jewish heritage, he had no interest in Judaism because of his fear of antisemitism practiced by Adolf Hitler as well as his concern that the same anti-Jewish attitude could easily spread to this country. His motivation, therefore, was to hide any association with Judaism or his Jewish heritage. He would refer to himself as an agnostic, claiming neither faith nor disbelief in God. As a result, my siblings and I were brought up Catholic.

The nuns in a Catholic school provided my education in kindergarten, first grade, and second grade. My brother and I had our first communion following our first experience with confession, in which the only sin I could come up with was fighting with my brother. I remember asking my mother what was the past tense of the word "fight" so that I could tell the priest "I fought with my brother."

After we moved to Bangor, my mother took all three of us to church on Sunday, and Paul and I took catechism classes. However, our involvement with the Catholic Church came to an abrupt end when the priest came to our house asking for more money. This unexpected additional financial request upset my father, who then completely severed our relationship with the Catholic Church. For several years thereafter, church was not a part of our lives.

We joined the Episcopal Church when I was in eighth grade, a development which had its origin at a cocktail party. It was at this social gathering that my father met Reverend John Brett Fort (for his own reasons he preferred to be called Mr. Fort). He was the priest at St. John's Episcopal Church, the only Episcopal congregation in Bangor. They struck up a rather deep conversation about religion in general. Being an agnostic, my father was not so sure about the existence of God, but he did believe that Jesus was a real person who traveled around Jerusalem spreading the importance of love, sensitivity, and the need for people to care for one another. He firmly believed in the teachings of Jesus Christ and their value in creating and maintaining a stable interdependent society.

He did not believe in the apocalyptic events described in the Bible such as the resurrection, the parting of the Red Sea, or Jesus's ability to walk on water. Instead, he felt such events were the result of the absence of the written word during Jesus' time, an absence which allowed bards and storytellers to make up stories as they entertained their listeners around campfires. A similar origin of storytelling was popular in ancient Greece when *The Iliad* was created. While authorship of *The Iliad* is routinely attributed to Homer, it is well known amongst scholars that the story may have started with Homer, but the embellishments of the story, of which there were many, were the result of the inventive imaginations of traveling bards who were storytellers. The process allowed these people to create whatever interesting events they could come up with to capture the imaginations of their listeners. Stories were then passed from one commune to another, altered by subtle and not-so-subtle embellishments by multiple storytellers.

What my father discovered at this cocktail party with Mr. Fort was that the two of them completely agreed with one another in regard to the importance of religion. He was most impressed by the openness of this minister of religion to a more realistic and explicable description of the origin of classical religion. As a result, my mother and we three children became active members of St. John's. In fact, my brother and I became acolytes, chosen to be part of the important midnight services every Christmas Eve. All three of us underwent confirmation classes and were confirmed in the Episcopal Church.

Kathy in 1959

There was a monthly Sunday youth group of high school students in which I furthered my relationship with Kathy, my girlfriend and the secretary of the youth group. She became my wife eight years later in a ceremony at the same St. John's Episcopal Church with Mr. Fort officiating. It is most interesting that a seemingly insignificant introduction of a Jewish psychiatrist to an Episcopalian minister led to a five-plus decade love affair between two people who believed in and continue to follow the teachings of Christ, minus the storytelling embellishments created over many years by bards focused on maintaining the interest of their listeners.

Politics

I do not recall any dinnertime conversations involving politics. The only time politics came up for discussion in our home was in casual conversations with my father, generally focused around presidential elections. As valuable as Dwight Eisenhower was to our victory in Europe through the D-Day invasion of Normandy in 1944, my father was a fan of the opposing candidate for president, Adlai Stevenson, because of his elevated intellect. He felt Eisenhower was an excellent military tactician, but he felt Stevenson had a stronger general intellectual ability to better understand the complexities of running the entire country. Alas, my father did not get his wish and the country survived.

As a sidelight of Eisenhower's presidency, he experienced a heart attack while playing golf. This brought to the public's attention the importance of heart disease and its prevention as practiced by Dr. Paul Dudley White, a cardiologist at the Massachusetts General Hospital – perhaps creating the seed of my interest in cardiology.

Another presidential election that triggered a conversation with my father occurred in 1964 between Lyndon Johnson and Barry Goldwater. The Vietnam War was at the top of newscasts, and Goldwater was proposing the defoliation of the Vietnam jungle with nuclear weapons. My father and most Americans were frightened away by Goldwater's thinking regarding nuclear warheads, and Johnson won by a landslide. The presidential competition between John Kennedy and Richard Nixon also triggered the interest of my father, who felt that Kennedy and his advisors were functioning at a very high intellectual level, higher than Nixon's advisors. Therefore, he felt strongly that Kennedy should be our next president. This time he got his wish.

By far, my father's favorite politician was Franklin Delano Roosevelt, whom he credited with the ending of the Great Depression that had begun in the late 1920s. His admiration for FDR and his successful programs to stimulate the economy arose from his proposal for the New Deal, the promise of which led to FDR's election to president in a landslide in 1933. FDR felt that only the federal government could bring this country out of the depression. He succeeded in this assessment by passing laws leading to banking reform, job creation, emergency relief programs, and agricultural stimulation. He ensured his re-election for three more terms in the office of presidency by passing a second New Deal, creating Social Security, union protection, and aid to farmers, as well as the creation of jobs for migrant workers.

Military industrialization in preparation for the high likelihood of our involvement in World War II further ramped up the economy in spite of the efforts of some politicians for the US to remain neutral. This abruptly ended with the Pearl Harbor attack by the Japanese on December 7, 1941. Our declaration of war against Japan then extended to Germany, because Japan and Germany previously had signed a treaty that mandated the declaration of war by Germany against the United States in the event of the declaration of war by the US against Japan. Hence, the Japanese bombing of Pearl Harbor brought the United States immediately into a two-front war. The first American troops arrived in the British Isles in January 1942, but nearly a year passed before they saw action.

FDR, unfortunately, lived at a time when there were no effective antihypertensive medications other than a rather ineffective diuretic, based on mercury. As a result of this absence, FDR experienced systolic blood pressures as high as 350 mm Hg. It was thus not surprising that his health deteriorated and he passed away from a cerebral hemorrhage on April 12, 1945, unfortunately preventing him from seeing the end of World War II.

To a great extent, it was FDR's long-standing struggle with hypertension that led to my father's compulsive attention to his own blood pressure, checking it every night before going to bed. Even though he stayed on top of all the latest psychiatric literature, he also diligently read the *Journal of the American Medical Association*, updating his knowledge of new antihypertensive agents. The first such medication that caught his eye was a new drug called MER 29, created by the major pharmaceutical corporation, Merck. Unfortunately, this agent was found to have a side effect of causing blindness, thankfully discovered before my father made any progress in getting himself on it.

Shortly thereafter, in 1960, Merck came out with Methyldopa, known as Aldomet, which my father took for fifteen years before it started to interfere with his liver function. He then switched to a new beta-blocker, Propranolol, which remains an effective antihypertensive treatment to this day, although diminished in popularity by newer beta blockers.

The only other political issue my father felt strongly about was Medicare. While he thought some form of insurance for the elderly was needed, he did not want Congress to be involved, fearing that further government control of the practice of medicine would follow. Alas, my father was prescient, as you will see when I discuss my run-in with Medicare involving a serious disagreement with the policies of Medicare directed at the prevention of coronary artery disease.

Hugs

I grew up in New England, and therefore absorbed the prevalent personality of New Englanders, which is considerably more reserved than what is practiced in the Midwest and perhaps many other regions of the country. I suspect New Englanders' somewhat reluctant approach to establishing relationships has its roots in the seventeenth century immigration of most of our forefathers from England, which classically has been reserved when establishing new relationships until a closer familiarity of the new individual is established.

With religious conflicts in old England and discomfort within the English caste system separating royalty from both the elite and the working class, one never knew in old England whether one could be immediately confident of the safety or longevity of spontaneous friendships. Thus, in our family and our circle of friends, there were few or no hugs and kisses as a standard form of greeting. Therefore, in spite of all the love, support, and encouragement I received from my parents, there were no hugs when I returned home from school and no kisses even after extended absences. In fact, the only kiss I shared with my mother was when she said goodbye after helping me get settled in my dorm at Harvard my freshman year. And the only time I recall kissing my father was before his return to Florida after a hospitalization in Milwaukee for congestive heart failure, shortly before he passed away.

However, I can now report that I and my entire family have absorbed the Midwestern approach to greeting one another with hugs, now standing behavior upon returning from an absence. Even without hugs, I was always well aware of the emotional warmth of my family as I was growing up, and am happy now to combine that emotional family warmth with physical confirmation.

Chapter 17

Nurturing Women

I was very fortunate to be nurtured by three women who showered the men they loved with unprecedented love, caring, and support. However, despite the identical nature of their behavior toward their men, the subtext of their nurturing style had its roots in strikingly different back stories hovering under the surface.

Grandma Bertha's back story is uncertain to me because it was never discussed. I knew she left home in Budapest to take her two sons to other countries that had maintained access to higher education for Jews. . Her sons, André and Paul, wanted medical degrees, and the Hungarian government was severely restrictive for Jews seeking higher education in Budapest. Bertha was more than willing to usher them around Europe so they could accomplish their goals. Her determination to make her sons successful physicians reflected her strong personality trait of conscientiousness.

But what happened to her husband, Eugene? Why would she take her two adult boys and leave him in Budapest? I do not know the answer, but I do have enough clues to allow me to come to the conclusion that Eugene probably died of a heart attack, perhaps brought on by the stress of being a Jewish banker in a highly antisemitic environment prejudiced against successful professional Jews. My first clue leading me to this conclusion was the fact that he left behind his signet ring and cyanide suicide ring, both of which Grandma Bertha gave to my father. If Eugene had been captured by the Gestapo or had divorced Bertha, it is unlikely that he would have left these items behind.

Secondly, my father was always interested in the prevention of coronary artery disease, as indicated by his interest in cholesterol and hypertension extending over many years. There topics were often brought up while I was a teenager. He would compulsively check his blood pressure every night before going to bed, and we had many discussions over the dinner table regarding the control of saturated fat in our diet. In fact, he discovered one theory of saturated fat reduction which could be accomplished by neutralizing the effects of saturated fat on coronary arteries by eating more polyunsaturated fat. Since there were no cholesterol-lowering medications in those days, dietary adjustment was the only approach to an elevated cholesterol level.

The value of exercise in the 1960s and 1970s was unknown as the potent cholesterol-lowering intervention that is widely accepted today. In fact, my father was a maverick in his focus on cholesterol management to protect his own heart, because I recall attending an American Heart Association meeting in Houston in 1975 in which two very respected cardiologists debated whether cholesterol had any role whatsoever in the development of coronary artery disease. The truth of its role did not become known until about twenty years later, when scientists were able to break down the total cholesterol level into its two component parts: the bad cholesterol (LDL) and the good cholesterol (HDL).

While the total cholesterol level correlates poorly with coronary artery disease, the LDL cholesterol level correlates very closely and is an ongoing focus in my current work involving the prevention of coronary artery disease in my patients. I focus on aggressive lowering of the LDL to levels not seen since our infancy, which is now possible with statins and other medications. This has been possible since the approval of the first statin, Lovastatin, in 1985.

The average American has an LDL of 130, approximately 90-100 points higher than what it should be in the prevention of coronary artery disease in high-risk individuals. The third clue that my grandfather Eugene passed away from a heart attack at a young age was my father's experience with a heart attack in 1966 when he was only fifty-five years old. Fortunately, it was a small heart attack for which he was hospitalized about a week. He was uneasy about this experience because he told me there was no such thing as a "small heart attack." All heart attacks were serious, making my father more attentive to cholesterol and blood pressure.

Now, with the information granted by coronary angiography, we do know that a blockage in a small artery can indeed cause a small heart attack, assuming there is no significant disease in the major coronary arteries. In my father's day, however, there was no coronary angiography, no balloon angioplasty, no stents. Therefore, his doctors sent him home to continue his careful diet and blood pressure monitoring. In addition, since blood clots were felt to play some type of role in coronary artery blockages, he was also discharged on warfarin, a blood thinner he took until his final days. While this medication gave him a sense of proactively avoiding the fate of his father, scientific data have since documented that warfarin carries no benefit at all in the prevention of heart attacks. Instead, we frequently use a milder blood thinner, a platelet inhibitor, Plavix, for this purpose.

As a result of his genetics and despite my father's careful diet and close blood pressure monitoring, he passed away from congestive heart failure resulting from progressive coronary artery disease.

The conscientiousness trait of his personality allowed him to live twenty years beyond his "small" heart attack. I am quite convinced that his motivation was stimulated by the unfortunate experience with heart disease in his father, who succumbed to it at a young age. It was an event that made it easy for Grandma Bertha to leave Budapest and ac-

Kathy and I beamed on our wedding day in June 1966, flanked by my mother, Rita.

company her two sons with uncompromising love through Italy, Scotland, France, and England.

My mother's back story behind her devotion to my father, and by extension to her children, had its roots in her early childhood. She was the middle daughter of loving parents living a comfortable, middle-class life in Endicott, New York, a small suburb of Binghamton. Her father, Franklin, was a domineering individual, very devoted to his Catholic religion and extremely opinionated in all issues open to debate. There is no question that the nature of his love was what we now call "tough love." This conclusion is confirmed by my mother's rebelliousness, as manifested most obviously by her decision to start smoking while in nursing school despite strong prohibitions against it by the nursing school administration. This led to a semester-long suspension. In addition, her rebelliousness was clearly demonstrated by her love affair and elopement with a foreigner – a Jew, no less – actions which she knew stood in marked contrast to the strong prejudices of her father.

In spite of his toughness, Franklin did have a soft spot in his heart, as revealed by his spontaneous gifts to me of small, individually wrapped sugar donuts, which he shipped several times to me when I was in college. These were sugar donuts from a favorite bakery of his and of my mother's in Binghamton. She remained close to her father and sisters despite her strikingly rebellious marriage. She visited Binghamton several times and even participated in a large Daley family reunion, taking along my brother and me. Such acceptance of her family obstacles is a reflection of the openness trait of her personality. Clearly, there was a strong undercurrent of family love among Franklin and his three daughters until his death from colon cancer.

My wife Kathy's back story is far more complex, perhaps because I was a classmate of hers for nine years and slowly became aware of her multiple family conflicts. This led to obstacles in her ability to confront external challenges. Her personality combined two traits: a high rating in conscientiousness that gave her a strong determination to rise above her broken family's poverty level; and a lower score in emotional stability because of the uncertainty and unpredictability of her mother's personality.

Kathy Kazmierczak captured my imagination and interest the first time I saw her. We were only eight years old, and I recognized a distinct look of pleading in her sorrowful, brown eyes framed by brown braids, capped by plaid bows. Full, determined lips, whose softness against mine would become apparent many years later, were balanced by her pleading eyes. She was standing against the back wall of our third grade classroom, making her the last student awaiting a desk assignment. Not only was she physically alone, but unbeknownst to me, she was also emotionally alone, finding herself in a new school with no friends. Making matters worse, this new school was a neighborhood school miles away from her home. She was living in a small apartment in a commercial district a few blocks from a movie theater on one side and a railroad station on the other – not a place for children.

Kathy looked lonely when I saw her standing by herself against the back wall of the classroom. Something was not right. It took many years, decades in fact, for me to learn what was going on in the mind of that little girl, who seemed lost among the other children around her. Her capture of my imagination started with this first encounter when I had the distinct feeling that she needed a friend and perhaps more.

It was Tuesday, September 2, 1952, the first day of school at Vine Street Elementary School in Bangor, Maine. It was a very special day for me because it was the first day of school in my new hometown, in which my family had arrived only three months earlier. It was an opportunity to meet new friends and a new teacher in a new school that had been built only the year before. I was excited to meet my new teacher, Mrs. Lucas, and I was excited to be in a new school with very modern architecture featuring lots of glass, unlike the usual brick-and-mortar schools elsewhere. My excitement gained outlet physically by riding my bicycle around the school yard, checking out all the nooks and crannies of this sprawling school and discovering the main entrance door, where we read the official starting time of the opening day's activities.

At the same time in another part of town, there was an anxious eight-year-old girl sequestered in her tiny commercial apartment looking out her window, seeing neither children nor playgrounds and wondering how she was even going to get to Vine Street School. Two different worlds were about to collide only twenty-four hours later. Since this elementary school was a neighborhood school in a middle-class neighborhood, most of the students walked to school or were dropped off by their parents. One day in the future, this particular neighborhood would become Kathy's neighborhood as well, but on this particular day, her emotion preceding the start of school was only apprehension, not excitement.

She could only dream about the layout of this school. Her apartment was too far away for her to walk to school or even explore its outward appearance prior to that first day. In addition, her mother did not have a car. Fortunately, her mother had a job as a dispatcher for a taxi company, and she was able to get a taxi to take Kathy to Vine Street School. However, her taxi trip to the school that day would not end on the school grounds. Instead, she made the driver drop her off, school bag and all, several blocks away so the other kids would see her walking to school, just as her future classmates were doing. This would allow her to be seen as one of the group rather than an outsider living miles away. Her need to belong was extremely strong, even at age eight.

She was so ashamed of her actual neighborhood in that commercial district that she refused to tell the teacher her address because of all the poverty it carried with it. She said she could not remember it, even though she clearly knew it.

It is difficult to imagine all of these thoughts percolating through an eight-year-old's brain, all alone, naturally shy, no friends for support. As distressing as her living conditions were, the hard part was keeping them hidden from everyone around her if she ever was to have any hope of becoming part of the Vine Street School community.

Several weeks following that stressful first day of school, Kathy's mother found an apartment on the third floor of a home on Sixth Street, only four blocks from Vine Street School. It was an easy walk, but more importantly, a walk peppered with other children all heading in the same direction. Her new home had an address she felt comfortable revealing to her teacher because it was located in the Vine Street neighborhood, complete with family homes and playgrounds, far from industrial buildings. She was also encouraged by the fact that her new neighborhood included other school-age children with whom she would become friends throughout her later elementary and secondary school years.

From her standpoint, life was now looking good from a physical standpoint, but not yet from an emotional one. She was not comfortable with her life inside her home. Her parents were recently divorced, which in itself was an embarrassment to Kathy, as evidenced by the following story.

An adult neighbor living near Kathy's new home mentioned to her that she had noticed in the *Bangor Daily News* a divorce which had occurred between a husband and wife named Kazmierczak. Kathy denied this couple was her parents. She told the neighbor it must be a different Kazmierczak, as if little Bangor a city of 38,000, could have a whole clan of Kazmierczaks. If she had lived in the Polish section of Chicago, she might have gotten away with this comment, but eight-year-olds do not have logic built into their brains as standard equipment. I am sure the neighbor was not fooled, but very likely felt sorry for Kathy and simply dropped the matter.

I mention this vignette to further emphasize the strength of Kathy's pride, which throughout her childhood she continually struggled to defend: first her address, next her parents' divorce, and ultimately a mother who was frequently demeaning, often disparaging, and never complimenting, all the while living at the level of poverty.

In addition, her mother's personality was mercurial. Love could not be counted on and anger was never far from the surface, even without provocation. Maternal closeness was rarely available and Kathy could never count on it. Fortunately, the household had a grandmother, Kathy's maternal grandmother, who was sweet and supportive. Unfortunately, her sweetness was tempered by developing dementia, which ultimately led to her confinement at the local state hospital, where she passed away.

There is a saying in life that things happen for a reason. In Kathy's case, her mother's physical and emotional absence led to more and more responsibility being placed on Kathy's shoulders. Magnifying this dynamic was the fact that she had a sister six years younger and a brother nine years younger, whom she had the responsibility of caring for while her mother was working three-to-eleven shifts. Kathy quickly learned how to babysit, pick up the house, feed an infant, and cook simple dinners on the stove out of necessity. Because all of the ingredients for whatever she was preparing for her meals were not always available in her apartment kitchen, she learned how to make substitutions, using items that were different, but similar in taste or texture to whatever she was preparing. To this day, Kathy has such eclectic cooking skills that after enjoying a particularly delicious dish, I frequently ask her if she can make it again. The answer is always the same: "Maybe, maybe not."

Recipes are not required accessories in our kitchen, "A little of this, a little of that." "No celery? No problem. We'll find something else crunchy." Somehow, her meals always come together, but all too often they are a one-off experience! In Kathy's world, the ingredients determine the recipe, not the other way around.

From a psychological standpoint, her mother's emotional distance, with its absent support and lack of encouragement, forced Kathy to develop alternative support from within herself and from teachers who offered compliments of her work at school. Kathy worked hard in her classwork, learned how to enhance her ability to memorize, and how to compliment herself with a pat on the back when she received good grades.

She learned how to interact with adult conversations by spending time with the landlady of her apartment building, who recognized the impact that Kathy's mother's absences were having on the child's development. Kathy's experiences during her youth clearly followed the proverb, "Necessity is the mother of invention," or as Plato phrased it, "Our need will be the great creator." These few words continue to be an important feature of Kathy's life to this day. There is no giving up, no turning back. She learned from mistakes and advanced with her successes.

After she left her unhappy home and went to live in a college dorm, Kathy desperately wanted to ultimately create for herself and her future family a home full of love, comfort, and caring — all of which started with our marriage and was passed on to our three boys. She learned through her early contact with me about the loving activities of Grandma Bertha and those of my mother. Her goal became continuing the same supportive behaviors she observed in these two women, passing on to me the opportunity to study hard during medical school, as well as her encouragement to overcome future challenges on my path to a successful practice of cardiology in Green Bay, Wisconsin.

Chapter 18

Kathy's Childhood Challenges

While there were a few moments of warmth in Kathy's early life, the overall trajectory of her childhood was definitely downward and at times teetered on disaster. It easily could have changed this optimistic, hopeful young girl with positive goals into a helpless youngster ripe for corruption and failure.

To understand Kathy today is to understand her inner strengths as a child; strengths that alone kept her on the correct pathway, navigating between proper and improper. Importantly, to understand Kathy today is to appreciate how childhood stresses have frequently filtered through to current experiences. She was a pillar of positive thinking arising from a foundation of vulnerability.

I do believe her future successes began with the roots of stability that were set down at the beginning of third grade, when we first set eyes on one another. Without a doubt, the person who had the greatest influence on Kathy during her childhood was her mother, but not in a good way. In fact, Kathy modeled her life to be anything and everything her mother was not.

In order to understand this rather bizarre relationship, I must begin with a discussion of Kathy's mother, her stresses, and her mercurial personality. First her stresses: Lena Inman was the older of two girls. Her father worked for the railroad and died suddenly of a pulmonary embolus when he was in his sixties. Lena's mother never entered high school and could neither read nor write nor tell time. Lena left Bangor and worked for a time in a Bath, Maine, shipyard called the Bath Iron Works, constructing ships during World War II while Kathy's father, Edward Kazmierczak, was in the army. Lena had a child out of wedlock during this period, unfortunately a "blue baby" who died at approximately thirteen months from congenital heart disease.

Lena returned to Bangor when the shipbuilding job ended and started working as a taxi dispatcher. She joined her sister, Louise, and their mother, who had been caring for little Kathy while Lena was living in Bath. Edward joined them later after his discharge from the Army. That made five adults (counting the grandmother) and little Kathy all in one small apartment! The living arrangement created immense pressures on Lena, including disagreements between her and her sister, which eventually led to Louise's departure to her own apartment. The stress of Lena's responsibilities in the care of her mother, whose lack of education was gradually joined by slowly progressive dementia, would have been an extremely challenging position for anyone.

Stress is an unavoidable fact of life and affects all of us in numerous ways. For some, the effects are internal: rapid heartbeats, palpitations, hypertension, fatigue, shortness of breath, and chest pain. For others, the effects are external with mood changes, irritability, impatience, or love withdrawal. Lena's response to stress fell into the withdrawal of love category, which was obvious to all her children who were unfortunate enough to find themselves within her presence at the wrong time.

Such was the case with Kathy, who, as the oldest child, could be blamed for any housekeeping shortcomings, arguments between siblings, or general duties left undone. There is no question that Kathy's mother was faced with multiple stresses: financial and interpersonal, highlighted by her divorce from Edward when Kathy was only eight years old. Even this divorce was conflicted, as reflected by Lena's continued caring for her ex-husband's needs. These included regularly providing him with lunchtime sandwiches and a physical relationship that lead to the birth of Kathy's brother, Steven James.

There was no dearth of stressors for Lena Kazmierczak, and any one of them could flare at any time. The common outlet manifested in a criticism of young Kathy, who was the ultimate outlet for blame, no matter what the stress was in Lena's life. What made life difficult for Kathy was the fact that her mother could at times be attentive and caring, such as she was on the first day of third grade when she braided Kathy's hair and placed plaid bows on the two braids. But Kathy never knew when the next "explosion" was going to occur, with shouting and mean comments. Such inconsistency of moods proved impossible for Kathy to form any compassionate relationship with her mother. Kathy's response to this inconsistency was to turn her attention inward, amplifying her own strengths, allowing her to successfully accomplish everyday responsibilities and devise her own future goals.

Because of her mother's inconsistency, to this day Kathy is uncomfortable with any friends who are inconsistent in their expression of friendship. Hot and cold responses in friends tend to push Kathy away. Within a few minutes of my first vision of Kathy standing alone at the back of our third-grade classroom, I sensed her discomfort as she faced new unknown and untested classmates, hoping to find a trustable friend.

Her unhappy experience in her tiny commercial apartment came to an end a few weeks after school started. Her mother had saved enough money to rent a third-floor apartment in a three-story home on Sixth Street, only a few blocks from Vine Street School. This allowed Kathy to walk to school just like all the other neighborhood children – no more taxicab deliveries. However, while the external turmoil regarding her arrival at school was now resolved, she still was experiencing major internal turmoil arising from her parents' divorce. The continuously empty chair at the table made her family feel incomplete. It was an extremely unsettling situation for Kathy, who desperately wanted to be part of a warm and cohesive family.

There were many internal conflicts for Kathy to deal with during her early years, chiefly arising from her mother's mercurial personality. It was often hidden just under the surface, with an unpredictable release of explosive behavior at any given moment. There was no physical abuse, but the verbal abuse was overwhelming.

Lena had much to be concerned about. She was now without a husband, while being responsible for two young girls after the birth of another daughter, Barbara, when Kathy was six years old. Living in an apartment that was barely within her financial means while holding down a low-paying job as a taxi dispatcher further complicated the matter. Lena can be forgiven for seeing no upside in the immediate or even intermediate future, but I find it impossible to forgive her for taking her insecurity and frustrations out on her children. Her behavior included sudden losses of temper, capped by angry requirements for the completion of multiple tasks of housework, undone items oftentimes more imagined than real. The verbal abuse was so oppressive that at one point, Kathy considered reporting her mother to Child Protective Services. However, she quickly nixed this option when she realized the consequences of such a revelation to the authorities could lead to the placement of her and Barbara in a foster home or even an orphanage, both of which were worse in Kathy's mind than continuing her attempt to adjust to her mother's unpredictable, raging temper.

In spite of the divorce's disruption on Kathy's internal calmness, worse was still to come. The divorce was not a conventional marital dissolution in which the parties separate and move on in two separate directions. This divorce was, in actuality, a divorce with second thoughts. They did indeed separate and live in separate apartments, but the two apartments were on the same street and only a few blocks apart. Lena continued to make sandwiches for her ex-husband every day, and it was Kathy's job to carry this food up the street to pass on to her father. Kathy's extreme sensitivity to outside appearances associated this activity with a high level of anxiety, because if a friend or neighbor should catch sight of her delivering food to her father, it would confirm her parents' divorce, which she felt obliged to keep hidden so that outwardly her family life would look like everyone else's.

As I look back at Kathy as a little girl who was facing all these dilemmas in real life, it is impossible to come away without the clear realization that this eight-year-old was emotionally functioning as an adult. She arrived at the conclusion that it was best to simply stay where she was and face the unpredictable rage of her mother. She was too young to understand adulthood or why adults behave as they do, all the while desperately struggling to maintain the outward appearance of a normal childhood. It was an effort that, at times, required the skill of a magician.

She did not even understand the meaning of stress nor how it affects behavior; she only knew how to tread lightly when confronted by her mother. This kind of stress is not supposed to be what childhood is all about. Quite the contrary, childhood is supposed to be an awakening to new beauty, new excitement, new wonder. She had no understanding of her mother's emotions, her stress, and no understanding of the relationship between stress and anger. She only knew that her mother had a bad temper. Furthermore, she had no adult support, no one to confide in, no one to explain the connection between stress and temper tantrums except perhaps through occasional, casual talks with the landlady.

Kathy weighed the alternatives for the future of her childhood with no meaningful adult guidance. Even though life was uncomfortable and uncertain, she had already demonstrated to herself that she had the strength of character to handle her mother's behavior. She was determined to do so until she was old enough to leave home, make her own life, and achieve her dream of one day creating a happy family with a husband who would love her, and children who would love and respect her.

And then in third grade, Kathy met me. I am sure at that age she did not see me as a potential husband. That was too far into the future. But she did see that I was part of a loving family, provided treats to classmates, and showed kindness to others. Psychologically, she felt reassured that, yes, in her midst there was a family that approximated the one in her dreams and that just maybe she would someday live in such a family. Little did she know that her time to leave home and its stresses behind would come sooner than planned.

On June 20, 1953, Kathy's brother, Stephen James, entered the world. Kathy was almost nine years old. Between Kathy and her mother's sister, Louise, Steve was well-cared for, went on to graduate from the University of Maine in geology, and became a longtime service manager of the Toyota dealership in Brewer, Maine. He serves as a leading member of the planning board for the tiny coastal town of Brooklin, Maine, where he and his wife, Kathy, now live. (This "Kathy" makes the second "Kathy Kazmierczak" in the Bangor region!)

The next addition to Kathy's family was her sister, Carol Estelle, when Kathy was sixteen years old. Carol's addition significantly added to Kathy's home responsibilities, because her aunt Louise had moved out to advance her own life's goals. With her mother's work schedule of three to eleven, Kathy took on the additional responsibility of babysitting three siblings after school. Every cloud has a silver lining, and the advantage to Kathy from this family responsibility was the opportunity to further develop her culinary skills as well as her home management knowledge to earn the Betty Crocker Homemaker of the Year award when she was a senior in high school. The cooking skills that she learned out of necessity are still part of her culinary repertoire today.

Meanwhile, Carol excelled in the judiciary field, achieving positions of court operations manager and clerk of courts in various locations ranging from San Diego to Utah to Virginia to Maricopa County, Arizona. She married René Camacho, who was a homicide detective in San Diego and a member of the special force there, monitoring the dangerous Mexican border before he retired.

Kathy's younger sister, Barbara, was only two years old when Kathy started third grade. She got lost in the family turmoil surrounding her parents' divorce, along with several moves to different apartments. The lack of maternal supervision and guidance led Barbara to an early life characterized by freewheeling, undisciplined behavior. This took a toll on Kathy, whose lifestyle was quite the opposite, with its compulsive organization and focus. Frequent arguments ensued, usually involving clothing that Barbara would borrow and not return, making Barbara's closet an unfortunate extension of Kathy's. Ultimately, Barbara matured and gained greater levels of responsibility and self-control. She married Stanley Witinski, a musician who played the organ in a small band, performing at numerous venues in Pennsylvania with Barbara supporting him in his travels.

As Kathy's responsibilities increased with the addition of Steve and Carol, she continued to adjust to a home life that can only be described as fractured, unmanaged, and misguided. She responded by refusing to allow it to subdue her emotional strength and determination to rise above her living conditions. She worked hard in school to obtain As in Latin, English, and chemistry. There was no maternal guidance behind these accomplishments, all of which were self-motivated. As if Lena's temper tantrums were not enough to challenge Kathy's path to a normal life, there was also a significant lapse in Lena's parental judgement. A striking example of this shortcoming occurred when Kathy was twelve years old. Lena irresponsibly placed Kathy and Barbara on a bus to travel from Bangor to Buffalo without an adult. The occasion of this trip was to visit her aunt, the sister-in-law of Kathy's father. To this day, the true motivation for this visit is still unclear since there had been virtually no prior contact between Kathy and this side of her father's family. Kathy cannot help but conclude that Lena wanted the girls out of the apartment in Bangor for her own personal reasons.

The unsupervised bus trip was only the beginning of an experience that was not only misguided, but more importantly, was illegal as indicated by the events that followed. The day after arrival in Buffalo, her aunt dyed Kathy's hair auburn brown and applied makeup to her face. She then dressed her in a cotton dress and heels. Once fully attired in this way, she teamed up with her sixteen-year-old cousin, similarly dressed and made up, and the three of them then took public transportation to what can only be called a "seedy" segment of Buffalo. Kathy and her cousin were told to simply stand at a street corner and "look pretty." Fortunately, nothing happened, but Kathy knew there was something improper and wrong about what was going on, and it was not long before they all returned home.

This experience was so inexplicable to Kathy as a naïve twelve-year-old from small-town Bangor that it was several years before she understood the promiscuity of this event and her involvement as a sexual foil, dressed in a pattern that was very close to child pornography. To further exemplify her aunt's lack of morality, Kathy's two-week Buffalo visit was cut to one week after her aunt was arrested for shoplifting. When Kathy's mother found out about this arrest, she dispatched Edward to bring Kathy and Barbara home. End of story, never to be repeated or explained.

That experience was followed a year or so later by an uncomfortable interaction with the husband of the landlady of Kathy's apartment. He invited a young teenaged Kathy to go to a movie with him, and presented her with the following opportunity: "If you scratch my back, I'll scratch yours." Kathy's body language screamed "no" as she looked fixedly straight ahead at the theater screen, and the mutual backscratching never occurred.

Kathy maintained very high moral and ethical standards in stark contrast to the lack of morality that surrounded her. She walked two miles on her own to St. John's Episcopal Church every Sunday, where she was baptized and confirmed, and later was elected secretary of the church youth group when she became of high school age. As a result of my father's relationship with the minister, I was also confirmed in the Episcopal Church and became part of the same youth group. It gave me another opportunity to spend time with Kathy while we were dating in high school.

In spite of her own poverty, Kathy had great empathy for other children whom she saw as being less well off than she was. For example, she felt sorry for another girl in her third-grade class whose clothing clearly reflected her poverty. Her appearance prompted Kathy to wrap up a red skirt and vest of her own, and place it anonymously on her classmate's desk. Kathy enjoyed an emotional reward the following day when she observed a simple smile on her classmate's face as she wore the gifted outfit. This sensitivity to and empathy for the plight of others less fortunate was part of Kathy's nature and was not a reflection of any religious teachings, since it wasn't until several years later that she began attending St. John's Church and studying the teachings of Christ.

After Kathy completed her freshman year at the University of Maine in Orono, there was an argument between her and Barbara, again over clothing that Barbara had taken and returned soiled and unwashed. The heated discussion brought their mother into the room. Lena told Kathy she was tired of the bickering and it was time for her to get out. Kathy called me in tears, wondering where to go. I called my mother, who asked a couple of friends if they might have room for a boarder, but neither was ideal.

My mother then called our minister, Mr. Fort, who had contacts at the University of Maine. He learned of an opening at Colvin Hall, a co-operative dorm in which the residents could work their way through the cost of boarding by sharing tasks such as housekeeping, diet planning, food preparation, clean up, dishwashing, and telephone duty, supervising the one and only telephone in the dorm. Mr. Fort's arrangement clearly was a gift from heaven. Kathy was now living on campus, no longer forced to pay for inconvenient ride sharing from Bangor to the university.

Chapter 19

Kathy and Peter

Kathy and I became acquainted in third and fourth grades, and actually went to a movie together along with a half dozen classmates, not a one-on-one date. We were assigned to different classrooms in fifth and sixth grades, and lost contact with one another. However, we were reunited in junior high school, which at that time involved seventh, eighth, and ninth grades. Since we were both enrolled in college prep courses, we shared most classes throughout junior and senior high school.

We started dating in eighth and ninth grades, and we learned much about one another, including our families. We agreed to "go steady" just before entering high school in tenth grade, which simply meant we would not date others. This was a decision made apparent to others by my signet ring on Kathy's finger. (It was the 1950s after all.) We continued steady dating in college, although agreeing that we could also explore dating with others. I was able to maintain contact with Kathy during our college years because I had a car at Harvard and was able to drive home for dates together about every six weeks, thereby making sure she would not forget me.

There were also times when Kathy would drive nearly four hours from Bangor, where she was commuting to classes at the University of Maine, to visit me at Harvard in Cambridge, Massachusetts, outside of Boston. We would enjoy a Harvard football game, a Boston Red Sox game, a Boston Symphony Orchestra performance, a Harvard class, or a chance to just spend time together. Our love blossomed during our four years of college, which brings me to December 22, 1964. It is neither a historical or religious date, but it is a very important date in our relationship. We were both juniors in college and had maintained a steady relationship for six years. We clearly had moved from friendship to love, from knowledge of one another to the understanding of one another, strengthened by caring about one another. Boyfriend-girlfriend no longer came close to describing our relationship, and thus it was time to move into the permanence of marriage.

We had never specifically discussed the topic, but it was definitely not far from our minds. I discussed my thoughts with my parents

Future married couples Paul and Nancy, and Kathy and me in 1961. The girls were wearing matching hand-knit blue vests.

Kathy and I had known each other since third grade when we finally tied the knot in June 1966.

and told them I thought Christmas time would be a perfect occasion to move our relationship to something more permanent. They had a friend in New York City, a jeweler who sent me a quarter-carat solitaire ring I liked. Then the planning of the surprise gift and its special question was left to me.

December 22, 1964, was a Tuesday, three days before Christmas, and I was home for the holidays. I made a reservation at the Somerset Hotel in Boston and a dinner reservation at one of its restaurants we had enjoyed in the past, The Hearthside. After two petite filet steaks

Our wedding day, June 18, 1966. From left, my brother Paul, me, Kathy, my parents, Rita and Andrew, and our officiant, Mr. Fort.

— no wine in those days — we went to Symphony Hall to hear the Boston Symphony Orchestra play Brahms Academic Overture and other classical pieces I was too excited to remember. Even though we had never discussed the exact purpose of this trip to Boston, Kathy knew something special was in the air. It was hard to sit and listen to the orchestra while I kept feeling the gift-wrapped ring in my pocket. The word "listen" is not accurate in view of what was going on in our minds, which was not focused on harmony, style, or the melody of the music. We were simply "hearing" the music as the excitement of the occasion gradually built.

At last, when the music was over, we went to our room, and as soon as Kathy saw the wrapped package the size of a ring box, she knew the following question would be, "Will you be my wife?" Since this day had been slowly building from that first encounter of two eight-year-old, third-grade students, she knew how to combine the word "Yes" with a passionate kiss!

When we returned home, my mother was excited, too, and told us she wished she had been a fly on the wall to witness the moment. Needless to say, I was glad she was not! We were married in St. John's Episcopal Church with Mr. Fort officiating on June 18, 1966. It was one month after Kathy's graduation from the University of Maine and one week after my graduation from Harvard.

In order to arrive at this point, we both had to get through college. Kathy chose to live at home to save money. She received grants, scholarships, and loans to help pay for her tuition, along with money that she had saved from work at a motel/restaurant, and later at the local telephone company as a telephone operator. She would travel back and forth during her freshman year with a few classmates from Bangor to the University of Maine's primary campus in Orono. This arrangement was difficult, because she had to go to school at the same time as everyone else in her car pool and return home only after everyone in the group had finished their schedules. Therefore, it made no difference what Kathy's classroom schedule was like.

Kathy's plan was to live at home until finishing her four years, after which she would have her teaching degree and be able to afford her own apartment. However, this plan started to break down just prior to the beginning of her sophomore year, and, as you may guess, her mother had everything to do with it. The argument with her mother and sister over clothing, noted in the previous chapter, completely eradicated that plan and, courtesy of Mr. Fort, provided Kathy with a dormitory room on campus.

It is important here for me to describe the subtext behind the importance of clothing to Kathy. Her sister Barbara's abuse of her clothing had nothing to do with fashion and everything to do with Kathy's persona. The importance of clothing for Kathy was to create the overall appearance she wanted to project to the outside world. It was important to hide her poverty and confirm that she indeed belonged in the company of her fellow classmates, and furthermore was worthy of their friendship. How she did her hair and how she dressed were very important to the image she wanted to project of someone who was not living in poverty. She, therefore, took excellent care of her clothing and made sure that everything she wore was clean and pressed. As Kathy

Our fiftieth anniversary portrait, taken in 2016
(Photo courtesy of Schroeder Photography, Ltd.)

matured, these issues became more and more important, which is why the argument with Barbara became so heated.

Then there was another crisis, again related to her mother, this time on the occasion of our wedding. The day before the wedding, Kathy's mother announced that she was not going to attend the ceremony, presumably out of embarrassment over interacting with my family. Kathy calmly told her if she was not going to be present in the church, she would have to call Mr. Fort and tell him herself because there was a special seat reserved for the bride's mother. Lena could not bring herself to call Mr. Fort and was in the correct pew at the right time for the ceremony. Later, after Kathy had changed into her "going away" outfit in the ladies room following our small reception, she was surprised to receive a hug from her mother, the first in her recollection.

Very clearly Lena was insecure, and there were several times during Kathy's youth, as well as her adulthood, when she felt her mother was jealous of her, a feeling that very likely contributed to the flares of anger toward Kathy. There, in fact, was much she could be jealous about, or at least envious. Here was Kathy becoming a bona fide member of the stable, successful Fergus family, and at the same time entering a life with a medical student who had a bright future — far from what Lena had experienced when she had been Kathy's age.

After our wedding and honeymoon in Bermuda, we lived in a small apartment in Bangor while Kathy worked for Head Start and I for the University of Maine chemistry department. We packed all of our belongings into the smallest U-Haul trailer and in September moved to a small apartment with only three rooms in Rochester, New York, for me to start at the University of Rochester School of Medicine. Kathy had her teaching degree and had obtained a teaching position for first grade students in an understaffed Rochester inner-city school. Kathy was charged with helping thirty-four economically challenged first graders learn the initial elements of reading.

With our immediate future settled, each with our own responsibilities, we began our new lives together. Like my father, I had major support while devoting attention to my medical school studies. My father paid my tuition while Kathy earned enough as a teacher to pay for our apartment and groceries. We were very happy. I was on my way to a career that I had been anticipating for four years, while at the same time basking in the joy of companionship with a partner who had been the love of my life for fourteen years already. That lonely, sorrowful, pig-tailed little girl looking for a loving family was now my wife, supporting me just as Grandma Bertha had supported my father as he was studying medicine long before.

My responsibility was to provide the warmth and security that was so depressingly absent in Kathy's unstable early life with her unpredictable mother. Like Grandma Bertha during my father's medical school education, Kathy did my laundry, my ironing, my meals, and the grocery shopping, giving me all the time I needed to do well in my medical studies. There was no discussion regarding the division of our labors. I was simply doing what I had always dreamt of doing during my college years, while Kathy was doing what she had always wanted to do now that she had left behind the turmoil of her mother's home and was able to focus her attention on her new husband.

The support she gave me during my educational years of medical school, internship, residency, and fellowship was only the beginning. She went further to support me with three sons while helping me cope with the anxiety of building a successful practice in cardiology, all the while developing and supporting the family of her dreams. Life was good.

Chapter 20

Our College Years

Our college years were very important for our emotional and intellectual development. While I was valedictorian out of 300 in my high school class, I knew I was not the smartest individual around, a conclusion confirmed by the presence of multiple high school valedictorians I met when I entered Harvard. What distinguished me and the reason I was accepted by Harvard was my emotional intelligence.

What is the difference between natural intelligence and emotional intelligence? Natural intelligence is genetically determined and characterized by the ability to quickly assimilate new concepts, integrate them with old concepts, solve problems with ease, and practice critical thinking in the process of absorbing these new concepts. Emotional intelligence is a learned skill because, to a great extent, it involves the development of self-awareness and social interaction as well as relationship management. Very simply, it is the ability to manage your own emotions and understand the emotions of others with whom you interact. The emotionally intelligent doctor is one who has a successful bedside manner, while a naturally intelligent doctor is one who is successful as a result of his technical ability and not by his warmth and compassion. In comparing doctors with emotional intelligence versus doctors with natural intelligence, just think psychiatrist as an example of the former and surgeon as an example of the latter.

Life is never black or white, meaning there are various combinations of the two types of intelligence. Emotional intelligence can be learned and enhanced through social interaction. It propelled me into college, helped me make my way through college, and encouraged me to prosper in medical school and further in my medical practice. Becoming successful with emotional intelligence requires a willingness to study hard, spend time to acquire knowledge, and practice the application of that knowledge. You learn what works and what does not. My developing social expansion led me to spend one morning per month teaching algebra to high school sophomores at Rindge Tech High School in Cambridge (later to be called Cambridge Rindge and Latin.) In addition, my enjoyment of music led to interactions with other musicians in the Harvard Band for four years.

I worked hard to get the grades I received in high school, college, and medical school, which enhanced my self-awareness in the emotional intelligence category. I lived in Hurlbut Hall my freshman year at Harvard, a dorm one block outside of Harvard Yard. My roommates and I shared a suite of four rooms and a bathroom.

Just meeting my roommates was an eye-opening, mind-expanding experience. There was Ken from Cherry Hills, Colorado, a suburb of Denver, whose father owned a major meatpacking company in Denver; Bruce from San Francisco, who loved jazz music and played the bass fiddle, frequently describing his high school girlfriend as a goddess; Lyle from San Diego, whose father was Jewish and mother Catholic, a very intelligent fellow who tried to figure himself out by dabbling in mind-altering drugs during his college years; and Howard from New York City, whose distinguishing feature was his feeble attempt to fit into the Boston environment by struggling to develop a New England accent.

Then, among these young men raised in cities of greater than one million population, was Peter Fergus from Bangor, Maine, population 38,000, arriving with my flute and my sadness over leaving my steady girlfriend behind. In spite of our obvious roommate differences, we got along very well and had many discussions, which opened my eyes to a lifestyle far more sophisticated than mine. Meanwhile, I taught them that a son of a psychiatrist could be well-adjusted and emotionally stable. Their prior experience with offspring of psychiatrists was the observation of maladjusted children who reflected failed experiments in child-rearing by parents who had been educated in child psychology.

Frequently, my roommates would tell me how "normal" I was. A large part of my normality was based on my ability to maintain a firm, long-lasting relationship with my girlfriend while, in the case of Ken and Bruce, they struggled with their current relationships: Bruce whose "goddess" seemed to be drifting away; and Ken, whose girlfriend was too simple and demanding.

My education in social awareness, courtesy of my big-city roommates, was equally matched by my educational experience provided by professors who were not only PhD-level educators, but also authors of the textbooks from which we learned. As an example, I learned about the interior components of a human cell in a biology course taught by a professor who helped develop the electron microscope. This instrument enabled the visualization of mitochondria, the nucleus, endoplasmic reticulum, lysosomes, etc., as well as their function. He wrote the textbook on electron microscopy that contained images of all of the inside structures of a single cell. This information was providing me with deep and absorbing knowledge into a region of medicine previously unknown to me, complete with pictures and the textbook author.

Then there was my exposure to Dr. James Watson who, along with Francis Crick, received the 1962 Nobel Prize in medicine for the discovery of the double helical structure of DNA. Not only did Dr. Watson give two lectures on DNA, he also gave each of the class members an unbound, yet-to-be published manuscript of his forthcoming book.

My sophomore organic chemistry class was taught by Dr. Louis Fieser, who wrote our organic chemistry textbook. As challenging as this course was, introducing us to the organization of carbon and hydrogen molecules in the construction and function of the human body, my most lasting and important memory of this class was one lecture by Dr. Fieser in January 1964. He had just returned from Washington, DC, where he had served on a panel appointed by the surgeon general in 1962 to establish the risk of cigarette smoking. We were given the results prior to publication of a paper that came to be called *Smoking and Health: Report of the Advisory Committee to the Surgeon General*. The study concluded that cigarette smoking was responsible for a 70% increase in the mortality rate of cigarette smokers versus non-smokers, not just from lung cancer, but also from coronary artery disease, emphysema, and low birthweight newborns of women who smoked during pregnancy. Only 44% of Americans believed cigarettes caused lung cancer prior to this report, but 78% believed in the relationship by 1968, just a few years after the report's release.

Hard at work studying at Harvard, 1963

Here I was, only a sophomore in college, listening to Dr. Fieser, a member of an august national committee, describing the actual statistics and conclusions which had the immediate effect of prodding Congress to pass a law one year later in 1965 requiring all cigarette packages to carry a health warning. It was a most impressive and unforgettable classroom experience. Smoking previously was considered a matter of individual choice, but the surgeon general's report expanded the issue of cigarette smoking into the public domain, empowering the government to take action to change individual behavior. My emotional intelligence provided me with fertile ground for the absorption of new information that I could expand through study and repetition into important knowledge.

Meanwhile, Kathy was developing her own emotional intelligence through increasing self-awareness and social expansion. She displayed mature self-awareness during her internal debate as a young child about whether to report her mother's behavior to the child protection agency by concluding that she was better off staying where she was and simply adjusting to the exigencies of her mother's behavior. The determination to succeed based in her personality trait of conscientiousness gave her the confidence to realize she was better off where she was at age nine. This decision created even more distress for Kathy because she was determined to keep her family situation secret from her friends and even me. In fact, her uneasiness about their living quarters in a second-floor apartment led her to clean the stairway with soap and water before each of my visits. This activity was totally unnecessary because I was focused on only one thing: getting up those few steps and spending time with my girlfriend.

A striking demonstration of Kathy's extreme social awareness occurred during adulthood when she observed a subtle change in the comings and goings of our next-door neighbors, leading her to predict a probable marriage breakdown. Four months after Kathy's prediction, the couple indeed filed for divorce.

Kathy worked hard to get good grades in high school, and her amazing memory was a big help. To a great extent, my discussion of her early years in this memoir is a reflection of that memory for all these events from long ago. What was important for Kathy was not only her long-term memory, but also the ease with which facts were able to get into her brain by way of memorization. Such was the case in English class, when she had no difficulty memorizing the twenty-six subordinating conjunctions as well as facts from assigned reading. Memorization also helped her match her A-grade in English with an A in Latin, for which she received a well-deserved diploma. But in no class was her memorizing skill more on display than the A she received in chemistry, a subject even now she describes as not having "a clue about." She simply memorized chemical formulas without the need to understand the principles underlying the equations.

Where memorization failed to help her was algebra. We had a rather fearsome-appearing male teacher who would walk around with a slight limp, waving his cane back and forth, and sometimes tapping his students on the leg. On top of his somewhat mean appearance, he had a challenging approach to math education. He would ask a student to stand at their desk while he required the calculation of a math problem. His refusal to accept a wrong answer added to the student's discomfort as he required them to stand there until they arrived at the correct answer. Nonetheless, Kathy received a B.

Kathy's prized memory even today has its unintended consequences. There are times when she acts like an "Irishman with a grudge." Unhappy moments, ill-chosen words by others, ill-meaning behaviors are not easily forgotten. For this reason, her childhood experiences occupy center stage in her memory and lead to new conflicts in life when current stresses are filtered through and magnified by these experiences from long ago. Based on my description of her childhood, it is easy to understand why this filtration of new experiences through old memories even now is an occasional source of stress.

While we have created together more and more happy memories over the years, the old filtration system has become a bit diluted and less of a distraction to her present day life. Nevertheless, her lifelong goal of creating a warm, loving family sometimes runs into various memories of conflicts with her mother — in the process disrupting current happiness and satisfaction.

Kathy did well in her college major of elementary school education because she loved children. She added another legal document to that diploma one month later: a marriage certificate that enabled us to move as a couple to Rochester, New York, to develop and grow our new lives together following college graduation.

Chapter 21

Mrs. Fergus Meets Mrs. Fergus

To better understand Kathy's tendency to allow her past stresses to creep into present day events, I need to go back to my discussion of personality traits, the so-called Big Five among psychologists. You may recall there are five personality traits: extroversion, agreeableness, openness, conscientiousness, and emotional stability. Kathy and the rest of my family all scored high in the first four categories as evidenced by their many friendships, ability to cooperate and be helpful, their flexibility and openness to new ideas, and their determination and dependability. But Kathy's unpredictable and chaotic childhood placed her in a category of emotional stability far from the more stable and emotionally structured experiences of the rest of my family.

The difference in emotional stability was never so apparent as when the new Mrs. Peter Fergus interacted with the older Mrs. Andrew Fergus. Casual conversations, even benign comments, often reached high levels of consternation in Kathy's mind during the most banal of interchanges. So how did this happen? Let's go back to personalities. My mother was very strong emotionally, a characteristic she demonstrated when she disobeyed the nursing school rules and took up cigarette smoking, or when she disobeyed her father's prejudices and went ahead and married a Jewish foreigner. Yet she had sufficient emotional stability to resume nursing school after her six-month suspension and further demonstrated the same stability by maintaining a warm relationship with her father despite his disapproval of her marriage. These qualities gave my mother a very high score in emotional stability.

It should come as no surprise that Kathy's emotional stability score was quite low with all I have described regarding her home life. How could it be anything but low in view of her mother's rapid-changing behavior, not to mention the uneasiness of her parents' peculiar divorce, one that seemed to be characterized by second thoughts? It is true that emotional instability can originate in one's genes, but unquestionably it is related to one's personal experiences to a great extent, such as the unpredictable interchanges Kathy experienced with her mother during her childhood.

As a result of these differences in emotional stability between my mother and Kathy, their conversations in front of me would create considerable confusion for me as I listened. I wondered just how Kathy's interpretation of my mother's words would later be presented to me. Here were two individuals whose early life experiences could not have been more at odds. My mother knew she could say almost anything she wanted, in any tone of voice, possibly finding her comments reprimanded by her father but never accompanied by the loss of his love. Kathy, on the other hand, experienced a very different home life in which she had to carefully parse or even suppress her words for fear of an emotional tirade from her mother. These tirades would include an implication of love lost and a vocal expression of anger, both focused on Kathy and ultimately leading to emotional instability.

Almost anything could happen when my mother and wife would get together because of the psychological concept of *transference* that played out as follows: If any of my mother's ill-chosen comments were to resurrect in Kathy's memory a long-ago argument with her mother, then the anger toward her mother in that ancient confrontation would be transferred and redirected toward my mother, who would then become the object of Kathy's anger. Such transferences would take place subconsciously, with no active awareness in Kathy's mind. It would leave me, the observer, in the lurch, wondering: "Exactly what just happened here?"

My mother and Kathy in the late 1980s

The analysis of transference psychology is in the realm of psychotherapists who analyze why long-ago experiences are affecting current everyday behavior. As a cardiologist and not a psychiatrist, I would respond to Kathy's concerns after these interchanges by explaining that my mother had always "shot from the hip" and felt free to say whatever was on her mind, without any filter. All I was trying to do was minimize the effect of my mother's comments on Kathy. Unfortunately, Kathy interpreted my attempts at mitigating the controversy as an attempt to defend my mother, thus putting me on the side of the enemy — obviously not what I intended.

As a result, I would back off and remain in what I hoped was a neu-

Enjoying a light moment in our kitchen, 2023

tral corner, not realizing that when it comes to mother-in-law and wife disagreements, all relationships are in an unending circle with no corners in which to hide. I would therefore back off and follow the old adage "happy wife, happy life." I would simply agree that my mother should not have said what she did.

No one can escape their past. The stresses and emotions of past experiences play a role in how we react in our present. Kathy was devastated by many of my mother's comments, while my mother had no idea of the effects of her words. The process of transference was taking place without the knowledge of either Kathy or my mother. Meanwhile, I was stuck in the middle, not understanding what was happening and trying to explain my mother's lack of diplomacy, only to find myself in trouble. Thankfully, it did not take me very long to understand what was happening and to stop defending my mother.

Meanwhile, my mother's comments and their fallout represented only the tip of the iceberg. Similar comments by non-relatives occasionally had unintended consequences after passing through Kathy's subconscious filter, tangling with her unhappy childhood experiences with her mother. Friends who were "hot and cold" in their interactions with Kathy were stark reminders of her mother's "hot and cold" behavior with its psychological consequences.

During one period in our marriage, we made contact with therapists who recognized and pointed out to Kathy and me that the stress experienced by her mother was very likely the cause of her irritable behavior. But no therapist took the next step to try to explain how Lena's stress and unpredictable behavior went on to affect Kathy's interpretation of current relationships in her life. That is until now, as I write this memoir and review the many experiences in Kathy's encounters with others. Many of these encounters have led to great uneasiness and anger in Kathy's mind, arising from a resurrection of her anger toward her mother followed by transference onto others.

I've observed many encounters, heard many evaluations of such encounters, and now I understand just how much Kathy's childhood unhappiness influenced her current attempts to enjoy her life and that of her children and grandchildren. We simply cannot escape the effects of our childhood experiences — good or bad. I was fortunate to receive plenty of love and support from my parents as I engaged in many opportunities in which my success was rewarded with positive reinforcement, propelling me to remain open to every challenge during childhood and even more so as an aspiring young physician.

Kathy's life experiences, on the other hand, have been subjected to modifications by ghosts from the past. As I faced the challenges and risks of new opportunities, I relied on the self-awareness provided by my parental support and the expansive social awareness provided by my college roommates. These well-developed traits of self-awareness and social awareness coalesced to increase my self-confidence — all contributing to the enhancement of my emotional intelligence.

As I developed my unique practice of cardiology, these traits gave me the fuel to proceed into new territory. But it was Kathy, whose strong love gave me the power to succeed in spite of the occasional challenges to her own emotional stability. She effectively burnished my own stability through her enduring love, without which my medical practice dreams would have remained unfulfilled.

Chapter 22

Medical School and Beyond

In ancient Greek society, the mind's education took place in three phases. Phase one was the accumulation of data, consisting of facts. Phase two addressed the combination of these facts into a pattern called knowledge. Finally, phase three involved the coalescence of these patterns of knowledge into a final phase called wisdom. All of my education through secondary school and college involved the accumulation of facts and their meaning. Entering medical school placed me on the doorstep of phase two: knowledge.

As I began medical school, I was about to coalesce all of my prior limited knowledge into a higher level called the practice of medicine. The challenge of expanding my previously acquired information sets into the knowledge of medicine was both daunting in its complexities and exciting in its challenges. This became apparent in my third year of medical school, which is when medical students actually interview patients and place our hands on their bodies. The knowledge gained by these actions then plants the seeds of wisdom for the future. I remember hearing a professor say early in my third year that it would not be long before I would be saying "in my experience" when describing a patient's symptoms to another doctor. The accumulation of such experiences is the foundation of wisdom, which future experiences expand and refine.

Every medical school has its own personality that determines its teaching style and focus on a particular aspect of medicine. Some schools graduate leaders in clinical research and laboratory investigation. Others favor preparing students to become experts in diagnostic medicine. Some favor surgical skills, and still others create professors to educate future students in the art and practice of medicine. These diverse directions are determined by the individual professors, part of whose job it is to create role models for students to emulate.

Even though there were many professors at the University of Rochester School of Medicine to emulate, the two individuals in my young career who had the greatest influence on my direction in medicine and whom I most wanted to emulate were not at this institution. Before I describe them, I would like to describe what I mean by "emulate." In the dictionary, the word "emulate" is often paired with its synonym, "imitate." However, the two words are far different in their subtext.

The first source of true emulation in my life was my father. I make this statement without any recollection of a specific action on his part to imitate. Instead, what I wanted to emulate in him was an entire persona, a total accumulation of actions and reactions that I observed – sometimes consciously, sometimes unconsciously – that led me to want to be like the person he was. As an example, I was impressed with the calmness he demonstrated while treating a patient in his office when I was observing the performance of electroconvulsive therapy (ECT). As part of the ECT procedure, a patient is given medication to paralyze their muscles so there will be no seizure activity when the electrical stimulus is applied to the brain. As a result, the patient's diaphragm does not work, and they are unable to breathe while they are under anesthesia for the ECT procedure.

A Life Worth Living

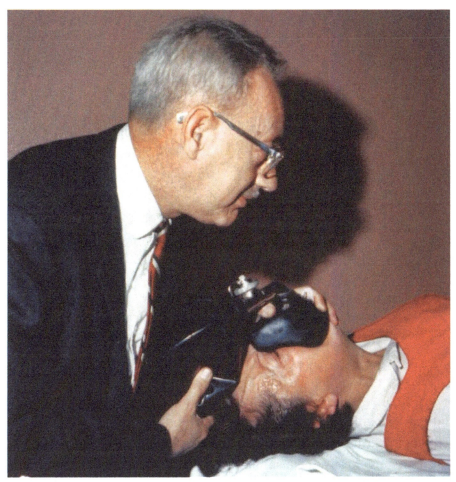

My father, Dr. Andrew Fergus, conducts electroconvulsive therapy (ECT) with the assistance of an Ambu bag, 1957. The bag valve mask provides respiratory support for patients during the procedure.

During this procedure, I observed my father very calmly breathing for the patient with what is called an Ambu bag. My father was completely calm during this procedure, in part because he had done it hundreds of times and was very confident in his ability to handle such situations. For me, I was nervous; the man was not breathing! I have subsequently incorporated the very same calmness in cardiology when faced with a patient in cardiac arrest, requiring my intervention along with the team assisting me. My calmness, in turn, extends to the whole team so that everyone can focus on their individual responsibilities. Watching my

My father (right) with his brother, Paul Forgacs, in 1981

father deal with a high-risk situation showed me that calmness means confidence. This was just one of many examples I observed in him that prompted me to assume a similar approach in the high-risk challenges I would be confronting in my future medical practice.

I see many patients recently hospitalized with cardiac problems. Because of the stress of their hospitalization, they do not have a good understanding of just what happened and what to do to keep it from happening again. In such situations, I have read their hospital charts, reviewed all of the tests they endured, and then faced the patient and their family saying, "We will figure this out" – calm and confident. My subliminal message is either I know what happened or I will get whatever additional information I need to explain everything that happened, and furthermore, how to fix it.

Throughout my career, the calmness and confidence I learned from my father has created for my patients a great deal of trust in me. Many won't follow recommendations of other doctors without clearing them with me first. It could be a change in medication. It could be the advisability of a non-cardiac procedure. It could be the decision to move to an apartment or stay in their home of forty years. They just want to hear me say, "It's OK."

In addition, my early life experiences at home made me aware of my father's love of my mother and the consistency of this love, which created a strong family cohesiveness. I learned that love and its corollary, patience, lead to long-term family stability. This awareness has led to my stable marriage for fifty-eight years and counting. In my professional life, I would remember my father's words, "Illness takes no holidays," when a hospital emergency would interrupt our home activities on a holiday. As a result, I am never alone in carrying out my responsibilities. I simply ask myself, "What would Dad do?" Importantly, my family also understands why I must go.

I am not describing a simple imitation of my father, but instead an overall form of behavior. Emulation is an absorption of another person's entire physical and emotional persona in response to any challenge, whether professional or personal. And when talking about calmness and patience, let's not forget about my father's position in the middle of my mother and my grandmother, acting as a referee and conciliator. I never heard a harsh word out of my father, or even my mother or grandmother in such complex settings, with all parties remaining patient. Calmness and confidence often lead to successful solutions and acceptable compromises. In my grandmother's case, numerous compromises led to various decisions on her living quarters. She started out by sharing a room upstairs with my sister, spent several months with her son, Paul, in London, and then moved to an apartment in St. Petersburg, Florida. She ultimately settled into an apartment in Bangor just above a dental office.

Before I get to my second source of emulation, I want to discuss the University of Rochester School of Medicine, its values, and three of its professors who had a substantial influence on me during my medical school years. It was the personality of Rochester that made it my first choice of medical schools to attend. There were several reasons for this choice. The psychiatry department was well-known for its documentation of the relationship between emotions and physical disease. As described in the movie *The Godfather Part III* by Don Corleone's priest, "When the mind suffers, the body cries out." The gastrointestinal department and the psychiatry department at Rochester previously had documented the relationship between emotional stress and peptic ulcer disease, thereby linking the mind and the body. It is a linkage that is an important consideration in my current cardiovascular practice.

My father took advantage of Rochester's expertise in psychiatry by frequently traveling the short distance from Canandaigua, New York, to Rochester for seminars in psychiatry. I was especially excited about the University of Rochester when I discovered at my interview that courses in psychiatry were an integral part of the curriculum during all four years. During these classes, we delved deeply into the importance of compassion and empathy when interacting with patients. We witnessed the importance of letting the patient tell their story as we learned the art and techniques of interviewing symptomatic patients. This helped the patient feel the most comfortable, without any interruptions by the physician or the insertion of leading questions. I could always document important details the patient may have inadvertently left out at a later time.

The danger of inserting questions in the middle of the patient's recollections is the possibility they may become distracted and leave out an important part of their history. As one of my professors told me early in my third year, "Let the patient talk and he will give you the diagnosis." To this day, in my practice and in the teaching I provide my nurses, this open, non-directed approach extends to the individual questions. Ask "What does your chest discomfort feel like?" Avoid leading questions such as "Did the discomfort feel like an elephant sitting on your chest?"

The University of Rochester's personality, with its focus on the human mind and how interacts with the body, perfectly matched my own preconceptions of the disease process. It made me a very happy graduate when I left to become an intern and could apply all that Rochester had taught me. I encountered numerous high-quality professors once I entered Rochester's School of Medicine, but there were three who were instrumental in directing my future interest in psychiatry and cardiology. The first was my first-year advisor, Dr. Arthur Moss, a cardiologist and electrophysiologist. He was an excellent teacher of general medicine, which is required of all medical students before focusing on a specialty. His teaching abilities were recognized by every student with whom he came into contact. He went on to gain fame as an electrophysiologist, specializing in the causes and prevention of sudden cardiac death. This culminated in his work developing the internal cardiac defibrillator, which allows for the elimination of dangerous cardiac arrhythmias anywhere a patient may be experiencing a cardiac arrest.

The second Rochester professor who had a great influence on me was Dr. George Engel, a psychiatrist. He introduced us to the depths and complexity of psychiatry and its importance in the physician-patient interaction regardless of specialty. Dr. Engel emphasized the importance of the first interview and the skill required to extract the important details of a patient's illness. The first series of lectures in psychiatry featured his production of a multi-year home movie about a young girl named "Monica." In each class about Monica, which lasted a full year, we watched her start out as an infant and then gradually become a teenager. Dr. Engle would lead a discussion of what we had just witnessed after each movie session. The segments would include frequent interactions between Monica with her mother, and sometimes of Monica's interactions with herself.

One such interaction involved innocent sexual self-stimulation when Monica, an infant only a few months old, accidentally placed her hand on her perineum and allowed it to linger there long enough for her mother to intervene by pushing her hand away. The subsequent class discussion focused on the fact that the nerves of sexual pleasure actually form during infancy. In a later movie episode, the psychiatrist asked ten-year-old Monica where she thought she might wind up as an adult, having lived all of her life in Rochester to that point. She responded by singing, "California, California here I come, right back where I started from," demonstrating the wistfulness and humor established early in our psychological development.

These were entertaining vignettes, but also very meaningful. Dr. Engel was also very interested in stress, and in this subject found himself closely allied with Dr. Moss regarding his interest in sudden cardiac death. Dr. Engel collected newspaper articles describing numerous examples of sudden death following an extremely stressful experience, such as a father arriving home to find his adult son collapsed and dead on the kitchen floor, only to pass away himself as the result of this shocking discovery. This example is part of Dr. Engel's biopsychosocial model of disease, relating biological disease to psychological and social stress.

Dr. Engel's presence at Rochester's School of Medicine was the result of his recruitment from the University of Cincinnati College of Medicine by Dr. John Romano, who also was at Cincinnati. Dr. Romano was very interested in the mind-body connection following his education at Marquette School of Medicine and Yale, where he studied both psychiatry and neurology. It was Dr. Romano's idea to require psychiatric education in all four years of Rochester's curriculum, reflecting his view of the importance of the mind-body connection. His intense interest in the teaching of psychiatry led him to become chief of psychiatry, where he achieved sufficient administrative influence to create a separate wing of Strong Memorial Hospital dedicated to psychiatry, forever to be called "R Wing" after Dr. Romano.

Every Rochester medical student's rite of passage was presenting their observations about an interesting patient whom we had studied during our psychiatry rotation to Dr. Romano and other psychiatry professors. My presentation was about a woman in her sixties who had received a head injury in an automobile accident on Route 66 in New Mexico. She had no visible structural injury by head X-ray or brain scan, but psychologically she was severely depressed and wound up in "R Wing," where I met her as one of my assigned patients. Part of the depression was the result of the timing of the injury — just before Christmas. Because of her depression, I learned very little from her and obtained all of my information about her from family members.

I also took a ninety-minute drive south of Rochester to her home and observed part of the reason for her depression: a stack of unopened Christmas presents in a corner of her living room one month after the Christmas holidays — enough to make anyone depressed. In a thirty-minute presentation to Dr. Romano, I discussed her psychological behavior before and after the accident. I shared with all my classmates, when it was their turn, some anxiety from standing before Dr. Romano with the hope that I was demonstrating a fair degree of competence. We all felt an overwhelming need to look competent and confident in this setting. Dr. Romano's opinion carried the same importance as that of the dean of the entire medical school.

Even though these three professors and others at the Rochester School of Medicine were outstanding teachers and physicians who made memorable impressions on me, none served to be my second physician to emulate. That second person did not enter my life until I became an intern at Boston City Hospital, where I met Dr. Bert Polansky. He was the attending physician on the medical floor where I was assigned along with other interns. He would arrive on our ward twice a week to hear us present our patients, ask questions about their diseases, and listen to his inimitable talent for sharing his well-earned wisdom. Dr. Polansky's peppered gray beard, unlit pipe, and white lab coat, made him the embodiment of a professor of medicine. Nevertheless, he was sufficiently laid-back to engage in small talk while awaiting the arrival of the other doctors for his attending rounds. He also had an engaging teaching style in which he would combine complex heart electrical abnormalities with amusing anecdotes from his personal experiences. The clarity of his explanations of heart disease stimulated my interest in cardiology, and his style made him a doctor I wanted to emulate.

Dr. Polansky especially enjoyed discussing the heart's abnormal rhythms, which he explored and explained in depth. His knowledge, calm demeanor, and confidence created the perfect persona of a cardiology specialist about whom I could say, "I want to be just like him." My desire to emulate Dr. Polansky, however, was based on more than just these characteristics. From the moment I first met him, he offered a personality unmatched by any of the medical professors at Rochester who had captured my admiration. He showed me charisma. As soon as he walked onto the ward, he appeared self-assured, fully into the educational process, open to questions, and readily approachable with answers. He was friendly, likable, and magnetic – exuding a level of competence that fostered complete trust, to which he added a charming and engaging personality. Once he entered the room, no one else mattered. There was no doubt in my mind: I wanted to be just like him and incorporate his charismatic style into to my practice of cardiology.

My observations of Dr. Polansky taught me a lot about charisma, but I needed to find a way to create my own style in my daily practice of cardiology. I therefore worked to combine the calmness and confidence I learned from my father with a touch of charisma from Dr. Polansky to create hope in my patients who are dealing with coronary artery disease or congestive heart failure. I accomplished my goal by making my presence in a room with a patient and his family psychologically meaningful. They already know that I am a specialist in cardiology. That knowledge is a given. How can I gain their confidence and trust by just walking into a room? I refer back to Dr. Polansky, whose appearance all by itself made him look like an accomplished professor. So, I make sure that I look like an accomplished cardiologist by wearing a suit coat complemented by a stethoscope around my neck and an engaging smile on my face. I acknowledge both patient and family, and ask the names of the family members. If I am a little late, I apologize and make sure that they know I will give this new patient all the time they need.

I then demonstrate my concern for this patient's problems by focusing all of my attention on them as they tell their story. My welcoming focus on the patient encourages their description of their story while my attentive listening encourages their focus on me. As a result, we are completely in synch with one another. I don't take notes; I don't type on the computer keyboard; I don't interrupt as they relate their story. I politely listen to family members if they choose to add information that is pertinent or correct any misstatements by the patient. After the patient has finished, then I ask a few questions to fill in any gaps or gain clarification of certain comments. I have already reviewed pertinent lab and X-ray reports, and personally looked at X-rays, echocardiograms, and stress tests. I then summarize my thoughts and conclusions, and discuss the most likely diagnosis and what we are going to do about it. I always maintain a spirit of optimism that I will figure out what to do after doing any required additional testing.

I patiently go over my thoughts, sometimes using the heart model in my office and always using everyday language in my description of what I think is happening to this patient's heart. I do not stand up until I have answered all questions and outlined a plan of action. In this process, I am showing my father's calmness and confidence combined with Dr. Polansky's charm and charisma so that the next time I see this patient and his family, I will be greeted with hopeful smiles rather than fear as I engage their full attention just by walking into the room. While I will never match the charisma of Dr. Polansky, I have achieved a modicum of charisma myself.

I do not have a professorial beard, carry an unlit pipe, or wear a white laboratory coat, but I do seem to approach a certain modicum of charisma when I walk into the nurses' station just as Dr. Polansky did when he entered the medical floor at Boston City Hospital. On these occasions nurses do not gather around me. I am simply talking with my nurse, Abby, oftentimes telling her an amusing anecdote about a visit with a patient. Not only does Abby start to laugh, but so do all the other nurses within earshot, as I now find myself the center of attention.

Chapter 23

West Roxbury to Green Bay

Upon finishing my internship and residency, I moved on to the Harvard Service at West Roxbury VA Hospital to focus on the diseases of the heart. This was my goal ever since crossing paths with Dr. Polansky. I anticipated an extensive experience in the treatment of heart disease because the VA Hospital in West Roxbury was the referral hospital for all veterans in New England who were experiencing cardiac symptoms. I was not disappointed.

I gained substantial experience in the technique of coronary angiography, the interpretation of echocardiograms, and the performance of cardiac stress tests. We lived in a 250-year-old New England colonial home in Norwell, Massachusetts. It was a thirty-minute drive to West Roxbury without traffic, twice that time during rush hour. The rent for this 5,000-square-foot, five-bedroom home was only $200 per month. We had two boys, Scott and Mark, an Old English Sheepdog, a nice yard, and a three-car garage. The low rent for such a nice home, however, arose from the three rooms at the front of the house that functioned as a working office for a general practitioner who used to live there until he built a new home further down the street.

Following his move, he rented the home to young physicians who would cover his practice on weekends in rotation with two established general practitioners. The young doctor renting the home could also make appointments for patients who were unable to leave work during the day and needed an evening appointment. With me being a cash-strapped cardiology resident making only $5,000 a year, such an opportunity seemed like a perfect exchange for an impressive home.

I did my own billing and my own record keeping. I even had hospital privileges at South Weymouth Hospital, which was a convenient stop on my way to West Roxbury and a facility where I could make rounds on the occasional patient I had to admit. The general practitioner's secretary would make appointments for my patients. After dinner, I would walk only a few steps from the kitchen into the office suite to see whatever patients were scheduled for me, usually only two to four. I would also be in the rotation for call on weekends, and on occasion I even made house calls.

In the process of this "moonlighting," I learned a lot about general practice patients and billing procedures. In addition, our landlord would collect ocean muscles at low tide from an estuary of the Atlantic Ocean that flowed just down the street from our home. He occasionally would offer a bucket of mussels to us. Kathy had always loved steamed clams, but was not familiar with mussels until we received these deliveries. Now they are one of her favorite seafoods, superseded only by lobster.

I started looking for cardiology practice opportunities during my second year at West Roxbury while we were living in Norwell. I was not interested in academic teaching opportunities. After four years of medical school and five years of postgraduate internship and residencies, I was ready to enter the real world of medical practice without the politics of academia. The much-respected weekly *New England Journal of Medicine* always had a classified section devoted to medical practice opportunities for young physicians in various specialties. On one occasion, my eyes fell on a two-year-old expanding cardiology practice in Green Bay, Wisconsin, that was looking for a partner to become its third member. The local hospital had recently built a catheterization laboratory and an open heart surgical suite.

I called the lead cardiologist, who informed me of the exciting potential of the practice. Kathy and I went for a site visit and an interview. Green Bay looked like a nice city, a safe place to bring up our children, and a very friendly population, discounting the fact that we were New England Patriots football fans and not fans of the Green Bay Packers. That would change, however, once we settled in Green Bay and I joined Cardiology Associates. It was obvious that we would become Packers fans.

Our boys actually ignored both the Patriots and Packers by insisting on the helmets of other teams simply because of their helmet colors. Meanwhile, we discovered that all the local news programs discussed in great detail everything about the Packers—their strengths, their weaknesses, their head coach (Bart Starr), their draft picks, and their stadium. You get the picture! We were brainwashed, and now all five of us are loyal Packers fans with Packers shirts and many other items of Packers paraphernalia. The Patriots – who cares?!

My move to Green Bay, in several ways, followed in my father's footsteps. After he finished his studies in psychiatry, he made a bold move to venture into a promising medical practice opportunity that happened to be in the state of Maine. It was a location he had never previously explored, having spent all of his time after arriving in America in various sections of New York State. Likewise, when I finished my education in cardiology, I found an enticing practice opportunity for the treatment of heart disease in which there was considerable potential for expansion, especially with my training in the new technology of echocardiography. My father moved northeast to uncharted territory in the state of Maine, while I moved westward to similarly uncharted territory in the state of Wisconsin.

We both felt the associated risks of such bold moves were justified by the practice development opportunities we would encounter. In addition, we were both young and had supportive wives and young families. If things did not work out as hoped, our youth as well as the youth of our families would allow us to pick up stakes and move onward, learning from our mistakes. However, our subsequent success confirms that we made the right decisions. Both my father and I thrived in our respective low-risk gambles.

It may appear as though I was in frequent conversations with my father to discuss risk/reward ratios associated with my move to Green Bay. However, at age eight, I was never aware of the risk he faced in his move to Bangor, nor did I consciously equate my opportunity as an adult to my father's move twenty-three years earlier. I do not remember asking for his advice, and I do not recall him offering his opinion, either. I think he knew that fatherly advice was unnecessary because it was obvious I had inherited his self-confidence and could make my own decisions. I instinctively followed in his footsteps because my genes guided me through a pathway parallel to his.

Chapter 24

1975 to 1995

I was very excited to start my new job as a cardiologist for Bellin Hospital, the only hospital in Green Bay equipped with a cath lab (short for catheterization lab) and an operating suite for heart surgery. I was also looking forward to teaching the other Green Bay doctors the value of echocardiography for the evaluation of left ventricular function and the heart's valves.

I had a number of telephone conversations with my new associates prior to arriving in Green Bay, and I was a bit dismayed to find out how often their patients were being referred for open heart surgery. Nevertheless, I accepted this fact and pledged to myself a goal of introducing a level of care that did not so often wind up in the operating room. I had a strong feeling there was a way of preventing coronary artery disease or treating it more conservatively.

However, the options for conservative management of coronary artery disease during my first decade in practice in the late 1970s and early 1980s were very limited. There were no medications to lower cholesterol. It was not even universally accepted that cholesterol played a significant role in the development and progression of coronary artery disease. There were many patients with heart attacks who maintained normal cholesterol levels when looking at the total cholesterol level. Researchers discovered many years later that the total cholesterol was actually composed of good cholesterol (HDL) and unhealthy cholesterol (LDL). It was the latter that actually correlated with coronary artery disease and not the undifferentiated total cholesterol level.

This is me in 1976, age 32.

In addition, there were only two primary medications to control hypertension, another important risk factor for the development of coronary artery disease. These medications were propranolol (a beta blocker) and hydrochlorothiazide (a diuretic). On top of the lack of preventive medications to reduce LDL and control blood pressure with the goal of preventing coronary artery disease, there were no medications to prevent angina in patients with active coronary disease other than the off-label use of propranolol. We were not allowed to prescribe medications for off-label indications during my internship and residency, but that prohibition was eliminated a number of years later.

At the beginning of my practice in Green Bay, along came diltiazem, a medication approved for opening narrowed coronary arteries and thereby improving the blood flow to the heart muscle causing the chest pain. It was approved for the treatment of angina, functioning as a vasodilator (opens blood vessels). It could increase the blood flow to the heart muscle when a blockage was responsible for the patient's chest discomfort.

As a result of these limited interventions, there was little I could do toward my hope of preventing coronary artery disease or treating its related symptoms outside surgery. In fact, coronary artery bypass surgery was the primary way of relieving debilitating angina pain. Hence, the focus of my new partners' frequent use of heart surgery. I simply needed to be patient while technology developed the tools that I would require to achieve my goal of prevention and early treatment.

I had the opportunity to use coronary bypass surgery myself during my second year in Green Bay, but in a completely different way than to simply reduce symptoms. This experience started with a patient named George, who gave me an opportunity to do something that had never been done before in Green Bay and rarely elsewhere. One day when I was on call, George entered the hospital in the throes of a heart attack that was affecting the lower portion of his heart, as shown by his EKG. His vital signs were stable, but he was still having discomfort and his EKG was clearly showing the acute phases of cardiac injury. It did not seem right to put him in the coronary care unit to wait things out, hoping the pain would go away, while allowing the injury to his heart to progress unabated.

At that time, the standard treatment for a heart attack patient was simply watchful waiting with tranquilizers, rest, and intravenous lidocaine, a medication to prevent dangerous heart electrical activity. I discussed with my senior partner my thought of performing coronary angiography on an emergency basis to identify the offending blockage, following which George could go up to the operating room for placement of a bypass graft to reroute his heart's blood flow around the blocked artery. He told me that it was my decision. I therefore did the only things that seemed right to me: I alerted the heart surgeon, called the cath lab team into the hospital, and safely performed coronary angiography, which revealed the offending blockage in George's right coronary artery. Once this blockage was surgically bypassed, the EKG returned to normal and George's angina pain resolved with no significant heart muscle injury, allowing him to return home a week later.

To fully understand the significance of what I accomplished with George, I need to step back several decades and describe the evolution of the treatment of heart attacks during my lifetime. When I was a medical student in the late 1960s, a patient entering the emergency room with a heart attack was admitted to a general medical ward. They would be treated alongside patients with numerous non-cardiac illnesses such as pneumonia, strokes, gastrointestinal bleeding, alcohol withdrawal, etc.

There were no intensive care units (ICUs) or coronary care units (CCUs) for extremely ill patients. The result of this lack of focus on the heart was an in-hospital mortality rate for patients with heart attacks of fifty percent, usually arising from sudden cardiac death caused by unrecognized heart rhythm abnormalities. This serious complication was due in part to the lack of nursing attention on a general medical ward, which usually had one nurse looking after eight patients, all of whom had different levels of complexity. It would therefore not be unusual for a nurse making her routine rounds to find a heart attack patient cold and unresponsive, having experienced an unobserved cardiac arrest.

Bethany Hospital in Kansas City, Missouri, built the first coronary care unit in 1962 when the awareness of such frequent episodes of cardiac mortality from electrical abnormalities became apparent. Now, instead of placing a heart attack patient among non-cardiac patients in a general medical ward, they were admitted to a dedicated unit of six to eight patients with only two patients per nurse, allowing much closer attention. In addition, a monitor electrically attached to each patient recorded every individual heartbeat. An alarm would sound if there were any EKG abnormalities suggestive of an impending cardiac arrest. The specially trained nurse would then be alert to such impending disaster so that she could either inject medication to stabilize the heart rhythm or use an electrical defibrillator to restore the life-threatening abnormality to normal.

Many lives were saved as the result of the buildout of CCUs in most hospitals following the experiment in Kansas City. On the other hand, many of these survivors suffered from congestive heart failure resulting from the heart injury caused by the blocked coronary artery. The damage occurred while watchful waiting was taking place in the CCU as patients received pain relievers, tranquilizers, and reassurance from doctors and nurses. The CCUs were minimizing the electrical risk, but not the mechanical risk caused by the lack of blood supply to the heart.

Cardiac specialists then noticed that many heart attacks were caused by a blood clot on top of a plaque, which prevented the heart muscle from receiving the proper blood supply required for its survival. This recognition led to the development of various medications that could dissolve blood clots and reopen the blocked artery. They were very successful, but unfortunately had the complication of dissolving protective blood clots elsewhere in the body, leading to bleeding in the brain and the gastrointestinal tract.

There must be a better way, it was thought. This "better way" came out of Zurich, Switzerland, in 1977, when cardiologist Andreas Gruentzig inserted a balloon-tipped catheter into the blocked artery of a patient experiencing a heart attack. By inflating the balloon, he was able to compress the plaque and blood clot, thereby reopening the artery, restoring the blood flow to the heart, and stopping the heart attack. This news created enormous excitement and optimism among cardiologists with the knowledge that at last we could actually stop a heart attack in its tracks, preventing heart muscle injury and subsequent congestive heart failure in the process.

However, everything comes with a price, and the price for this balloon angioplasty procedure was the fact that the blockage returned within a few months thirty percent of the time. Thus, attention then directed toward the development of coronary artery stents, which very simply act as metal scaffolding to hold the artery open long term. Intensive research into the structure and best material making up these stents ensued, as well as the search for various types of medication to coat the stents and prevent their re-narrowing. The routine use of stents in the twenty-first century has reduced the in-hospitable mortality rate from fifty percent in the 1960s to one percent in the 2020s.

Today's current hospital heart attack protocol explains this dramatic improvement. Instead of a patient being admitted to a general medical ward, they go directly from the ER to the cath lab, where a stent is inserted within sixty to ninety minutes. This prompt action saves the heart muscle and stabilizes its electrical system. Patients frequently can be discharged to home within one to two days.

What I accomplished with George anticipated by decades the value of quickly restoring the circulation to the injured heart muscle. I only had bypass surgery at my disposal as the modality for achieving this goal with George, while currently it requires only the insertion of a 2.5-mm to 3.5-mm stent without surgery. I was fortunate to be born early enough to participate in every incremental improvement in heart attack care described above.

Next, I wanted to expand my new procedure, called echocardiography, which I had brought to Green Bay. It was an ideal technology to determine the strength and size of the heart muscle, and evaluate the status of the heart's four valves. We were often using echocardiograms for these purposes in Bellin Hospital, but what about the hundreds of patients in small hospitals in nearby communities that did not have the equipment or technologists to perform echocardiograms?

I trained a technologist in the early 1970s in the performance of echocardiograms at Bellin. One day, we got to talking and together raised the possibility of outfitting a van with a lift to carry an echo machine to these outside hospitals. This would enable us to perform diagnostic procedures at remote locations on patients who had been identified as needing more sophisticated evaluation of their hearts. I felt that identifying patients with heart disease in outlying hospitals would also enhance the number of patients referred to our group at Bellin for further evaluation, which might include coronary angiography, electrocardiograms, and cardiology consultation.

Since echocardiography was new and not understood by most of the physicians at these outlying hospitals, I went to numerous medical meetings to explain the theory behind echocardiography and the advantages of early treatment of the diagnoses revealed by this procedure. The physicians were most interested, and I received approval from the state to perform such transport procedures. There was no charge to the hospitals. All I needed was a room. I obtained a loan from the bank to purchase an echo machine, the van, and a lift to get the echo machine in and out of the van. I then hired a technologist whom my Bellin technologist trained to perform the echo procedures. We called our service Mobile Diagnostics. My partner did all of the paperwork, including the billing, and I would read the echocardiograms. I would walk out to my mailbox every evening to pick up the videotapes with images for me to review in my home office.

I then felt that ultrasound could be used for more than visualization of the heart, and therefore spent time learning from a medical school classmate who had moved to California to practice radiology. He gave me training during the week I was there in interpreting ultrasound studies involving the abdomen and pregnant women, which turned out to be so popular that all of these hospitals eventually purchased their own equipment and hired their own technicians once they realized the value of these procedures. Simply put, my success put me out of business!

Meanwhile, my partners were not as enthusiastic about my mobile business as I was, even though it did lead to increased referrals. Moreover, mobile diagnostics was not the only point of contention in our cardiology practice, which had added two more cardiologists. I felt there was considerably more room for expanding our practice, and I felt that our practice, which was a monopoly, did not create any motivation to expand. Although we had a warm and respectful relationship, I was becoming concerned that our group was not being aggressive enough in regard to accepting patients who might be in need of our services; patients, for example, who were admitted to other hospitals with a small

The Green Bay HeartCare sign outside of our new location on the far west side of Green Bay, directly across the street from St. Mary's Hospital Medical Center, 1995.

heart attack and were stable, but not necessarily out of the woods. In short, I felt the practice of cardiology in Green Bay needed competition, and concluded I was the one to provide it, especially with my differing approach to heart disease focused on prevention and early detection.

As a result, I made the decision to break away from the group in 1984, dissolving the monopoly, and creating competition in the local practice of cardiology. I was confident that cardiology could reach new heights in the Green Bay market, and I was also confident that my style of compassion, warmth, and empathy in my patient care demonstrated during the preceding decade would continue to bring referrals when I created my own practice.

I called my new practice Green Bay HeartCare (GBHC). I started this project with the help of one nurse, Betty Stevens, and one secretary, Mary Pensis. Betty was an outstanding nurse with extensive experience taking care of sick patients in the intensive care unit at Bellin. While I was seeing hospitalized patients during my first nine years in Green Bay, she frequently had an opportunity to observe my compassionate style of treating heart patients and witness their positive responses to my care. As I started to seriously consider forming a new cardiology practice, emphasizing my personality, Betty was immediately all in without my asking. In addition, she had strong organizational skills, which played a large role in developing the efficient framework in our new building on the west side of town. Green Bay is very much an east-west city, bisected by the Fox River. Bellin and St. Vincent Hospital were long-time anchors on the east side of the river, while St. Mary's Hospital Medical Center had relocated from that same area to the far west side in 1963.

Meanwhile, Mary had been the secretary in my original office with my two partners, and was most impressed with patients' comments about the type of attention and focus they had received from me during their visits. As a result of Mary's familiarity with my practice style, she too volunteered to join me in my new venture. Like Betty, she had excellent organizational skills, arranging my schedule, hiring additional secretaries, and guiding me in the purchase of the necessary equipment for her duties. She also took on the responsibility of helping my office staff adapt to our new computer network, which we installed later.

Bellin administration was supportive of my initiative because they saw the advantage of competition in creating opportunities for expansion of their involvement in cardiac services. During the first year of my breakaway, Bellin allowed me to see patients in their Treatment Center until I was able to purchase my own office from a general practitioner who was near retirement, a purchase which included the furniture. It did not take me long to replace all of the 1950s-style furniture which had long ago passed its prime. I also purchased new office desks and exam tables to which I added a treadmill, nuclear imaging equipment, and an echocardiogram machine, as well as a small blood test analyzer to measure patients' cholesterol levels. I was now able, within my office, to do the preventive work of which I had long dreamed as well as the early treatment of patients with heart symptoms.

My practice thrived to the point that I was able to buy a second treadmill so I could do two stress tests at the same time. I needed to become certified in nuclear medicine and isotope handling in order to perform nuclear imaging as part of the stress test. This education required a one-month course divided into four one-week sessions in different parts of the country, following which I received my nuclear license. In the process, I also hired the necessary technicians to perform the nuclear procedures as well as a technologist to perform the echocardiograms. I expanded my operation to involve a receptionist and a billing secretary.

Ultimately, I even went back to the mobile business and leased a large truck in which I placed a nuclear camera, and hired the necessary employees to perform the procedures as well as drive the truck. The stress tests would be done on a treadmill provided by the outlying hospital I was visiting, following which the patient would be transferred to the truck for the nuclear imaging. One day a week, however, we would park the truck just outside the back door of our office building in Green Bay, thereby allowing me to do three nuclear stress tests at the same time. As you can imagine, we quickly outgrew our rather small building. It was originally designed for four general practitioners, but not for all of the ancillary equipment I had installed.

I purchased some land not too far from my home or from Bellin Hospital, and hired an architect to design a building to house my practice as well as other businesses. However, the cost/benefit ratio for this project did not look as good as I had hoped, thereby prompting me to look elsewhere for my expansion.

It just so happened that there was a four-story office building going up directly across the street from St. Mary's Hospital. During construction, it had been marketed to a number of specialty practices interested in expanding their reach to west Green Bay and St. Mary's Hospital. However, just as the building was being completed, President Clinton's health care plan proposed that more power be given to primary care physicians in deciding when and where referrals for specialty care should be given. A number of the specialty physicians from east Green Bay had given verbal commitment to lease space in the new building, but because of the uncertainty created by President Clinton's health care plan, they all backed out.

A local realtor involved with this building knew I was in need of a larger space for my practice and thought the space on the west side of Green Bay would give me a competitive advantage. It would allow me to expand heart care beyond east Green Bay and into the west side, specifically involving St. Mary's Hospital, thereby completely eliminating the monopoly created by cardiology's focus on only one hospital (Bellin) in east Green Bay. I liked the future potential for my practice on the west side, sold the land I had bought for a new building on the east side, and purchased the basement, first floor, and fourth floor of this new office building. Later, because of my concern that the rest of the building could wind up in the hands of a chiropractor, I expanded my mortgage to take over the entire building. I installed a large sign out front identifying my practice as Green Bay HeartCare.

GBHC had offices and exam rooms on the second floor and exercise testing, laboratory, and further exam rooms in the basement. I leased part of the first floor to a transcription service I used for dictation, and the rest of the first floor to a plastic surgeon from St. Mary's. I designed and hired carpenters to build a cardiac rehabilitation center on the fourth floor complete with a cushioned running/walking track and additional space for exercise equipment. My own physical therapists provided the supervision, as well as gentle yoga instructors who were focused on exercising the elderly.

We also had an auditorium with a digital projector for lectures about heart disease and its prevention, and we even had cooking pods for demonstrations of healthy food preparation. I leased the third floor to the St. Mary's physical therapy program. My building was thus completely leased out. Our new sign out front confirmed to the community that Green Bay HeartCare had arrived! Life was good.

Chapter 25

Green Bay HeartCare

G reen Bay HeartCare's physical presence began with my purchase of a new building at 1727 Shawano Avenue on the west side of Green Bay, but its personality did not develop until we created an interior space designed in every way to reduce the stress of those entering with heart disease. Our office building was a four-story, box-like commercial structure with tan masonry. Not terribly interesting except for one feature: tall, welcoming windows encircled each of the four floors to which we added a stylized red heart above the entrance door. There was little I could do to change the exterior except to receive permission from the Green Bay City Council to erect a larger-than-usual sign announcing Green Bay HeartCare to passing motorists.

The far west end of Shawano Avenue was becoming a healthcare concentration featuring St. Mary's Hospital Medical Center directly across the street from our Green Bay HeartCare building and a nursing home just west of the hospital. Prevea Clinic had added a major multi-specialty clinic to the back side of the St. Mary's Hospital building in the late 1990s. It was space that had comprised the original hospital building when it was built in 1960, and had stood largely unused for several years. Prevea later moved those clinic operations into a new four-story building a block to the west at 1860 Shawano Avenue in May 2022.

Unlike the exterior of our building, I was in complete control when it came to the interior. Most medical practice interiors are designed to be functional and low-maintenance, which by default creates a sterile uninteresting environment. Instead, I wanted our environment to be comfortable and relaxed, more like a living room to counter the stress most people feel when dealing with heart disease. We decorated GBHC's waiting room with wall-to-wall carpeting, papered walls, plastered ceilings with indirect lighting, upholstered furniture, side tables with lamps, and artwork on the walls. It indeed could pass for anyone's living room.

The same carpeting and wallpaper with additional artwork extended

The Green Bay HeartCare waiting room, 1995 (Photo courtesy of Ryan Photography)

This was the entryway to the diagnostic testing area on the basement level of Green Bay HeartCare in 1995. (Photo courtesy of Ryan Photography)

into the hallways and exam rooms, complete with continued plastered ceilings and indirect lighting. Comfortable, upholstered chairs for patients and their family highlighted the exam rooms. In our lower level, used for exercise testing and diagnostic procedures, I decorated the walls in the entrance hallway with large, nine-foot vertical photographs of polar bears. Scattered throughout the rest of the lower level were more large photographs of zebras, bears and birds, as well as forests and wildflowers. This nature motif, created by renowned wildlife photographer Thomas Mangelsen, continued into our fourth floor cardiac rehab center for exercise and education.

To run GBHC's unique operation, I hired nurses, secretaries, an office manager, nursing assistants, physical therapists, and even yoga instructors to teach gentle yoga for the elderly. Only individuals who shared my passion for the psychological aspects of heart disease were hired, giving patients the same warm, caring, empathetic attention, no matter which floor of our building they found themselves.

The most important contributor to my goal of expanding the psychological care of my patients was the addition of Linda Halverson, a PhD psychologist, who had written her doctoral dissertation on women and heart disease. She came to me indirectly from a primary care physician, Vernette Carlson, in Daggett, Michigan. Dr. Carlson recognized the importance of psychological care in her primary care practice, but did not feel she had enough patients in need of Dr. Halverson's extensive cardiac experience to hire her full-time. She contacted me to see if I wanted to share in her employment. I arranged for an interview, and even before Linda and I sat down to talk, she knew from her tour of our office that she had found a home for her professional life.

My Green Bay HeartCare official portrait, 1996

There was no need and no time for Linda to share her skills with Dr. Carlson. After exchanging thoughts during our interview, we both knew we were a perfect match for one another, and a month later she was a most welcome member of our staff and a very important contributor to the personality of GBHC. We were on our way to creating a cardiology practice unmatched in the state of Wisconsin, a practice with a full-time PhD psychologist available to address the myriad of anxieties, stresses, and depressions people experienced in trying to come to grips with heart disease, whether from postoperative stress or the challenges of living with congestive heart failure and its attendant physical and dietary limitations.

Linda put her own unique stamp on just how far we could go in giving patients the emotional attention they were craving very quickly after arriving at GBHC. She routinely made her presence known to our cardiac rehab program, talking to all of our patients, face-to-face, about any emotional problems resulting from their hospital experiences, whether from a heart attack, heart surgery, coronary artery stenting, congestive heart failure, or atrial fibrillation to name a few frequent issues. Then, those she identified as needing ongoing care received appointments to see Linda in her second-floor office as many times as needed.

Her patients loved her because of her warmth, compassion, and understanding, including her knowledge of many aspects of heart disease. She taught them how to relax using controlled breathing, focused imagery, and meditation, to which she added reading material. Linda became indispensable to me and my vision of what an ideal practice of cardiology should look like. Sadly, after seven years with GBHC, Linda passed away in a boating accident. The uniqueness of her value in a cardiology practice and the large void her absence created are reflected in the numerous compliments I still receive from her patients even twenty years after her passing. Her unique value is further confirmed by the fact that I, unfortunately, have been unable to find anyone to fill her shoes.

Green Bay HeartCare Expands

After focusing on the emotional issues surrounding heart disease, I turned my attention to expanding our practice outside of Green Bay. To this end, I contacted John Goodman & Associates, a cardiology practice management firm known for creating detailed assessments of cardiology practices and their potential for expansion. The firm's representatives arrived in Green Bay to see exactly what our strengths were, and then did a geographical statistical analysis of the nearby communities including their populations, age distribution, the number of potential referring physicians, and the frequency of heart disease within this population. This data proved invaluable for my future plans.

Thanks to these statistics, I now knew the proper proportion of cardiologists to the overall population of a region such as northeastern Wisconsin, as well as the required number of cardiologists relative to the number of primary care physicians. I knew beyond a doubt that Green Bay was well short of the required number of cardiologists, as well as the inadequate distribution of its services to outlying regions. As a result, I was certain there was a market for my services in Marinette, a city of about 12,000 residents located forty-five minutes north of Green Bay. I could expand my previous involvement in this city, where I had been seeing patients only once a month in a room provided by the local hospital. I would see patients who were unable to make the drive to Green Bay for consultation, follow-up, and needed testing. One of my eighty-year-old patients in Marinette illustrated this limitation when she told me she could not make an appointment to see me in Green Bay until her son could get time off from his job in Texas to fly to Wisconsin and pick her up for the relatively short drive to Green Bay!

Primed with the statistics from John Goodman & Associates, I had sufficient data to assure me that I could expand my practice in Marinette to see both local patients as well as patients who lived further north beyond Marinette into Michigan's Upper Peninsula. I therefore initiated plans to open a full-time, full-service practice of cardiology, five days a week with consultations, follow-up visits, exercise testing, echocardiograms, and cardiac rehab. I leased half of a new building that was being constructed just for us, providing GBHC with 2,600 square feet. I then hired a full-time staff to enable our patients to receive the same level of care available in our Green Bay office, accompanied by the same relaxing decor.

A year after my commitment to Marinette, we had a grand opening ceremony to which I invited the mayor of Marinette, who presented me with a key to the city in recognition of my provision of this enhanced level of care. I also hired a full-time cardiologist for this office, assisted by my staff. Meanwhile, I would drive there myself once a week to see my patients. Green Bay HeartCare's expansion to Marinette occurred in 1997, only two years after we opened our Green Bay practice at 1727 Shawano Avenue.

Speaking to local dignitaries in Marinette, Wisconsin, at the 1996 groundbreaking ceremony for a building that would become Green Bay HeartCare's second home in northeast Wisconsin.

GBHC Expands into St. Mary's Hospital

While I was working on expanding Green Bay HeartCare to Marinette and beyond, I started working with St. Mary's Hospital CEO Jim Coller and Larry Connors, one of his vice presidents. I offered my support for the development of a cath lab at St. Mary's, thereby breaking Bellin's monopoly on cardiac services among the three Green Bay hospitals. As I write about these events, it seems like each of the transitions was an easy progression from Green Bay to Marinette to St. Mary's Hospital. That was not the case at all.

First of all, Bellin administration quite naturally did not like the loss of their monopoly for the care of patients with advanced heart disease, and accused me of driving up the cost of cardiac care through an unneeded second cardiac cath lab in Green Bay. The theory was that both Bellin and St. Mary's would then have underutilized cath labs, and as a result would have to increase their charges in order to break even on their multimillion-dollar investment in equipment. Bellin's concerns made their way to the *Green Bay Press-Gazette*, where I was criticized for supposedly driving up the cost of cardiology services.

However, thanks to my research and resulting statistics, I knew the potential future demand created not only by the population on the west side of Green Bay, but also the underserved significant population in Marinette and regions further north who would find St. Mary's location near US Highway 41 on Green Bay's west side more accessible than Bellin's location on the east side in the middle of the city. Therefore, I told the *Press-Gazette* reporter that Bellin was being shortsighted and not taking into account all the statistics I had compiled. These statistics clearly demonstrated the expansive potential demand arising from the communities north of Green Bay.

The next controversy came from St. Vincent Hospital, which along with St. Mary's is part of the Hospital Sisters Health System (HSHS). At the time, they were sister hospitals operating under separate management and still somewhat competitive with each other. (They operate more like distinct campuses of the same hospital today with a shared CEO.) St. Vincent was much larger than St. Mary's and already had supporting staff for specialty services, including coronary artery bypass surgery. St. Vincent thus felt that if HSHS was going to expand into high-tech cardiac services by way of a cath lab, it should occur at its location. However, HSHS leadership in Springfield, Illinois, recognized the need for St. Mary's to lead the way in the expansion of cardiology services because:

1. St. Mary's had its own need for service growth and enhanced respect.

2. HSHS leadership recognized the same statistics that had driven me regarding the population north of Green Bay, which would make St. Mary's west side location a more convenient destination from a geographic standpoint.

3. St. Mary's had a coincidental opportunity to hire an outstanding internist to initiate and expand its new hospitalist service, providing 24/7 in-hospital, physician-based patient care. Ashok Rai, MD, was the perfect person for this job given his drive, knowledge, and stimulation by challenges, especially an opportunity to create something new.

There was only one catch: Dr. Rai would not come to St. Mary's and create a safe haven for high-risk cardiac patients unless there was a cath lab on site for completing their evaluations and planning their treatment. Therefore, his needs, my needs, and the hospital's needs coalesced so it was St. Mary's and not St. Vincent that received the go-ahead to build a state-of-the-art cath lab. (Dr. Rai's skills were quickly recognized, and he rapidly rose in the HSHS and Prevea Clinic hierarchy, becoming the president and CEO of Prevea Health, the largest health system in Green Bay. Ownership of Prevea Health was a complicated arrangement in which St. Vincent, St. Mary's and the Prevea physicians had shared stakes in the business.)

Over the years, I have also benefited from Dr. Rai's ongoing support of my unique approach to heart disease. In spite of this victory, I had more problems to deal with. My two invasive cardiology partners were reluctant to use St. Mary's cath lab because there was no heart surgery capability on site, such as what Bellin had for evaluating high-risk patients. We solved this concern by agreeing to perform catheterizations at St. Mary's only on patients who were not considered high risk and not likely to turn into emergency situations. I then led the way by doing the first cath procedure at St. Mary's on a priest who had stable, but bothersome angina. He was shown by his risk factors to be unlikely to require bypass surgery or stenting. In fact, the coronary disease which I discovered during his catheterization could be treated with medication.

During the first six months of the cath lab's operation, St. Mary's CEO Jim Coller told me of his concerns that the number of catheterizations was not living up to budget. I discovered that my partners were unnecessarily labeling patients "high risk" when this designation was not appropriate. Therefore, they were inappropriately transferring these patients to Bellin for catheterizations. I had numerous discussions with them and described all the patients I had felt comfortable performing catheterizations at St. Mary's without complication. Gradually, their fears and concerns dissipated, and the cath lab volume at St. Mary's quickly reached budget.

I knew it was just a matter of time before we would encounter the need for stenting at St. Mary's. When balloon angioplasty and stenting first became frequent interventions at Bellin, all the cardiologists performing these procedures would contact a heart surgeon to be on standby and request an operating room kept open while the interventional procedure was being performed, just in case the interventional procedure was not successful. However, it did not take long before the heart surgeons were not happy just sitting around doing nothing, and the interventional cardiologists also quickly recognized that we rarely experienced the need for such emergent transfer of a patient from the cath lab to the operating room. There was a very simple reason why surgical standby was no longer necessary: We knew which patients were high risk for interventional procedures and which were low risk. As a result, following their catheterization, these high-risk patients were referred for elective coronary bypass surgery on another day, at St. Vincent or Bellin, while low-risk patients proceeded immediately to their stenting procedure at Bellin without the need for surgical standby.

To initiate our stenting program at St. Mary's, we used an algorithm to allow us to determine the stent risk for each patient based on their coronary anatomy. First, we did not even consider stenting until the cath lab staff had the experience of 100 routine cath procedures. Next, I called six hospitals in the United States where stenting procedures were being performed safely without surgical services on site. This confirmed that St. Mary's would not be an outlier, the only cath lab in the country to do such procedures without surgery in the same building.

I then put together a list of scenarios that would reflect high-risk conditions for coronary interventions that might require bail-out by a heart surgeon. Such lesions included a left main location, placing two-thirds of the heart muscle in potential jeopardy, lesions within a sharp bend, stenoses at a branching point, or arteries that are totally occluded (blocked). I presented my plan to the executive committee at St. Mary's, and they granted permission to begin the stenting program. Coronary interventions at St. Mary's then became a reality and were quickly accepted by our patients.

I received major assistance in my preparation for a cath lab at St. Mary's from Dan Doran, the first person St. Mary's hired to turn the million-dollar hardware into a functioning cath lab. He interviewed vendors for the equipment, and hired the necessary nurses and techs to bring the cath lab to life. He also was instrumental in helping me identify other hospitals in the country that were performing stenting procedures without surgical standby on site, enabling me to make a strong and successful case for receiving permission from the executive committee to initiate our stenting procedures.

Dan taught his team members well, allowing me to feel the confidence I needed to gradually expand our invasive and subsequent interventional cath lab program. Whenever I had a concern, he was my "go to" person to solve it. I needed to make sure the nurses in the intensive care unit knew what we were doing in the cath lab and what to look for as potential post-procedure complications including chest pain, hypotension, and cath site bleeding. The education of the nurses was very easy because they were already familiar with many cardiac emergencies associated with heart attacks and heart disease complications. They were very excited to now be part of the rapidly developing invasive and interventional treatment of heart disease, just like what was happening in larger hospitals. St. Mary's level of respect in the community thus blossomed by its inclusion with elite hospitals.

Coronary Artery Disease Prevention

Once I had the hardware set for early treatment of patients presenting to St. Mary's Hospital with acute cardiac symptoms, I turned my attention toward the prevention of coronary artery disease, especially in view of the fact that, even with all these treatment advances, heart disease remained the most common cause of death in the United States. In addition, I had the weapons to treat hypertension and hypercholesterolemia (high cholesterol in the bloodstream), as well as the statistics to document the value of weight control and regular exercise.

My interest in prevention originated from a well-known statistic that twenty-five percent of patients who experience a heart attack or succumb to sudden cardiac death had no preceding cardiac symptoms. So, how to find these asymptomatic, high-risk individuals? It is one thing to sit in front of a patient who has been experiencing cardiac symptoms and simply allow them to tell their story without interruptions. As the saying goes, "Let the patient talk and they will give you the diagnosis." But how could I find the patients who were on the verge of a life-threatening event despite having no symptoms?

From my readings in 2004, I learned about calcium scoring of the coronary arteries, a painless CT scan of the heart that quantifies the amount of calcium present in an individual's coronary arteries. The simple reason this measure of calcium is important is the fact that the only way calcium gets into the coronary arteries is for coronary plaque to get there first. Therefore, if a patient's CT scan shows a large amount of calcium, I know they have a large number of plaques. Specifically, if a patient has a calcium score of zero and is over the age of thirty-five, I can conclude that they have no plaque and therefore are at virtually no risk for a heart attack.

On the other hand, if they were to have a score greater than 1,000, I know they have ten times the likelihood of experiencing a heart attack or sudden death. Armed with this information, I would schedule a nuclear stress test, and if it was abnormal, I would proceed to coronary angiography, which would reveal their coronary blockages. I could then insert needed stents before these blockages could cause a life-threatening event. If these studies did not show severe coronary disease but only moderate disease, then I could focus my attention on risk factors, aggressively improving them to prevent that moderate disease from becoming severe.

The obvious statistical value of the calcium score was not being addressed in other Green Bay cardiology practices. I knew it was up to me to make this procedure happen. I therefore worked with the radiologists and administration at St. Mary's and explained the value of calcium scoring in the prevention of coronary artery disease mortality. The only problem was the fact that health insurance companies were unaware of the benefits of calcium scoring as well, and thus did not cover the cost of the CT scan required for the determination of the calcium score, which at that time was $700. I knew this out-of-pocket expense would stop patients' interest for this procedure in its tracks. I talked with Mr. Coller about this roadblock, and he convinced the radiologists to decrease the price to $250. However, that was not enough of a reduction, and I had only a very few patients who would agree to pay for the procedure.

Solutions to problems can come from many directions, and for calcium scoring the solution to my problem came from Appleton Cardiology, where they were charging only $50. The physicians there recognized the downstream value of identifying patients with coronary disease and its control by subsequent treatment. My decision became easy. I simply referred my patients to Appleton Cardiology for their $50 scans, an easy solution. Problem solved! After I joined Prevea Clinic and Dr. Rai found out what I was doing, his competitive spirit led him to get St. Mary's to reduce its price to $49.95.

The frequency of obtaining calcium scores has exploded in the years since. Its value can be demonstrated by my experience with one of my patients. I had been taking care of this man for many years, and had guided him through coronary bypass surgery and multiple stents. During one routine visit, he told me that his fifty-five-year-old son had recently died suddenly of a heart attack with no preceding symptoms. I asked him if he had any other children, to which he told me he had another son five years younger. I told him I wanted to see his son, at which time I ordered a calcium score that came back at 2,400, placing him in a very high-risk category. A subsequent stress test was abnormal and coronary angiography showed triple vessel disease requiring four stents. Here was an apparently healthy man with no cardiac symptoms only weeks to months from sudden death like his older brother. It was a classic confirmation of the value of calcium scoring.

This discussion of early diagnosis brings me to how I approach patients' cholesterol profiles. The standard therapy for the management of a patient's LDL cholesterol (the bad cholesterol which correlates closely with cardiac risk) is to bring the level below 100 if the patient has only one risk factor such as hypertension. (The average American has an LDL value of 130.) On the other hand, if a patient has had a heart attack, the goal is to push the LDL well below 70, aiming for the 30s, where it is when we are infants. However, when I see a patient with a high calcium score but no abnormality on a stress test, I know there is no need for further cardiac intervention. Nevertheless, there is a strong need for aggressive risk factor management to prevent progression of the coronary disease documented by the elevated calcium score.

For this type of patient, my reasoning goes as follows: if an LDL goal below 70 is good for prevention of a second heart attack in a patient who has already had his first heart attack, why not use the same aggressive LDL goal of <70 to prevent the first heart attack? In addition, a moderate level of calcium in the coronary arteries may not prompt any further testing, but it still indicates a significant amount of coronary plaque. This thereby justifies similar aggressive risk factor management to prevent progression of that moderate disease to severe disease. These risk factors include high LDL cholesterol, hypertension, diabetes, obesity, stressful life style, and lack of exercise, all of which can be optimized with close follow-up every six to twelve months.

GBHC sponsored annual screening clinics for $20, during which my nurses would ask about family history and perform tests for blood pressure, blood sugar, and cholesterol, the results of which could be analyzed to determine a patient's risk profile for having a heart attack well in advance of a real one. Such patients could then be advised to seek attentive risk factor management by their family doctors or me.

A side effect of my close follow-up of high-risk patients is that it allows these patients to feel comfortable calling my nurses any time they start feeling exertion-related discomfort in their chest, jaw, or arms, or if they start feeling short of breath from activities that never previously gave rise to any breathing concern. They know all they have to do is call my office and they will find a nurse to listen. The benefits of close follow-up and attention to risk factor management are reflected in the large number of patients whom I and my staff have been following for decades and are now in their eighties and nineties.

Chapter 26

Changing Healthcare in Green Bay

A lot was happening at the same time I was devoting so much attention to developing my practice at 1727 Shawano Avenue and expanding it across the street to St. Mary's Hospital as well as northward to Marinette. Storm clouds were gathering on three fronts:

1. Changes in the distribution of healthcare in Green Bay
2. My interaction with Medicare's Office of the Inspector General
3. My own health issues regarding my back.

Let's start with the changes in how healthcare was being provided in Green Bay. There were only two local cardiology programs from 1984 through the early 2000s: Bellin's Cardiology Associates and my Green Bay HeartCare. Family practice physicians from independent clinics had a straightforward choice for their cardiac referrals: them or me.

However, that simple dichotomy was about to change, prompted by construction of a new hospital on the opposite end of Green Bay, Aurora BayCare Medical Center. The entry of an additional hospital into the competitive local medical environment led to three separate systems in regard to cardiology services, each attached to a hospital: Prevea Clinic was affiliated with St. Vincent and St. Mary's; Cardiology Associates was affiliated with Bellin; and BayCare Cardiology was affiliated with Aurora.

The combined St. Vincent/St. Mary's/Prevea organization hired three cardiologists; Bellin absorbed the cardiologists of Cardiology Associates; and Aurora hired two cardiologists. Each system had full cardiology services including cath labs, open-heart surgery, and diagnostic equipment – all with their required personnel. Each system had its own set of referring doctors after acquiring the local independent primary care clinics and building their own new clinics. They naturally would be inclined, if not required, to refer patients in need of cardiology consultation to cardiologists within their own system. Furthermore, a new Medicare policy played a role in determining the location of valuable testing equipment. The policy provided greater compensation for nuclear stress tests and echocardiograms when performed inside hospitals and not inside private clinics. That meant I had to transfer all of my technical equipment and the personnel required to run them to a hospital.

So where exactly did Green Bay HeartCare fit in as an independent cardiac entity with no formal tie to any of the three systems? In two words "fewer consults." I, therefore, had to make a move, and the only option was to merge GBHC into one of these systems: Prevea, Bellin, or Aurora. The choice was simple, but the process was not. For several years, Jim Coller (the CEO of St. Mary's Hospital) had been encouraging me to join Prevea, even as Prevea was already hiring three cardiologists, all of whom were focused on interventional stenting procedures. Jim felt the addition of all my patients into the Prevea system, as well as my ability to attract new patients, would be a significant benefit to its burgeoning cardiology program and prestige. I had turned down Jim's

The Green Bay HeartCare staff in 1996. I am in the middle row, just right of center, with Dr. Ghazwan Katmeh just left of center.

offer each time it came up previously because he only wanted me and not my partner, Dr. Ghazwan Katmeh.

I first met Dr. Katmeh twenty years earlier when he was a locum tenens (temporary provider) I hired through a search firm to cover my practice for ten days while I went to a cardiology seminar. He was practicing as an interventional cardiologist in a heart group in Kansas City, Missouri, and was looking for new opportunities. Becoming a locum is a nice way to explore other opportunities while getting paid for it. In that short ten-day period while he managed my practice, he was very happy, and my staff took note of the match between his style and my style. In addition, my patients enjoyed working with him, and thus, after a second locum visit, I offered him a permanent position which he accepted. He became a welcome addition to my practice, reducing my call schedule to every other night and every other weekend. I was also pleased with his compassion and concern for my patients.

Dr. Katmeh and I had a very compatible and successful practice going, but Jim Coller did not see us as a team and thus, each time he invited me to join Prevea, he did not include Dr. Katmeh. I simply could not jettison Dr. Katmeh after his twenty-year association with me. So, I continued the status quo for several years and simply worked with Jim to enhance the St. Mary's cardiac program.

In the multilayered conflict that I was dealing with: my own survival, the survival of GBHC, and the survival of my employees, the turning points came in several unlikely forms. In Dr. Katmeh's case, the turning point came from his mother, a resident of Saudi Arabia who had become ill. Dr. Katmeh felt he needed to resign from GBHC so he could spend time with her. He thus announced to me that he had found a position as director of the coronary care unit in a major Saudi Arabian hospital, complete with paid-for living quarters and a personal automobile.

I sent a long letter to his new chief pleading for him to delay his hospital appointment, at least until I could find a replacement, which was no easy matter. His new chief thanked me for my letter and sympathized with my needs, but explained that his needs were equally as demanding, and so Dr. Katmeh departed in early 2007. There is a well-known saying; "Every cloud has a silver lining," and my silver lining in Dr. Katmeh's unfortunate departure gave me the freedom to join Prevea without any guilt over leaving him, given the fact that it was he who was leaving me.

Meanwhile, Prevea had hired three cardiologists of its own, and when Jim Coller told these physicians he had recommended to the Prevea administration that I be hired, they were not exactly ecstatic. Instead of seeing me as a welcome partner to share the burden of the call schedule, they saw me only as a competitor entering Prevea Cardiology to rob them of their future patients. The incredible and inexplicable solution to their conflict regarding my joining them was to accept me into their program ONLY IF I would be willing to give up my night and weekend calls. Most physicians who want to eliminate daily and weekend calls are required to give up twenty percent of their compensation, and here I was being given that benefit for free!

My first thought was, "This is too good to be true!" My future partners were simply being too protective of their own patient referrals. They were unwilling to give up any emergency room patients who would have come to me every fourth night and every fourth weekend. I immediately accepted their proposed "requirement" and we moved on.

The next turning point occurred when Prevea and St. Mary's hired a practice management firm to help analyze their cardiac services and the future for those services. The analysis revealed that the three cardiologists did not share my passion for the prevention of coronary artery disease. In fact, they actually may have seen prevention as an impediment to the future expansion of their interventional practices, especially in view of my stated goal of keeping patients healthy and out of the cath lab. As a result, all three of them gradually left Prevea over a six-month period.

The final turning point occurred while Prevea's cardiology partners were moving on and another Fergus, this one named Todd, my son, was entering the practice of cardiology. Todd had completed his education at Harvard College, The University of Michigan, Scripps Mercy Hospital, The Medical College of Wisconsin, and a specialized interventional (stent) program at St. Vincent Hospital in Indianapolis. Subsequently, after Todd joined Prevea, the clinic went on to hire five more cardiologists: a nonintervention cardiologist, Jennifer Davis; two interventional cardiologists, Anas Sarhan and Simil Gala; an electrophysiologist, James Hansen; and a pediatric cardiologist Beth Medford. I became Director of Preventive Cardiology.

With my assimilation into Prevea agreed upon, it would appear my life was now stress-free. I had no call responsibilities, a partnership in a major medical clinic whose primary care doctors could freely refer patients to me, and a close affiliation with two major Green Bay hospitals in St. Vincent and St. Mary's. It all sounded good, but unfortunately, more storm clouds were gathering.

Chapter 27

The Merger

This second bank of storm clouds hovering over me in 2007 came from the complexities of joining Prevea Clinic. This move made perfect sense because of my prior relationship with St. Mary's Hospital, including my contribution to its gaining approval for a catheterization lab, coupled with my own desire to create a west side cardiology practice. Operationally, however, it was a different story, because my addition to Prevea was part of a package deal. It was not just me, but Green Bay HeartCare AND me. That is when things became quite complicated. As the saying goes, "the devil is in the details," and solving the complexities of these details required lawyers and accountants to help Green Bay HeartCare and Prevea move together.

In addition, GBHC had a sister corporation called Cardiac Imaging Center (CIC), which owned our nuclear equipment, echo machine, and laboratory equipment in both Green Bay and Marinette, as well as contracts for their maintenance and repair. Furthermore, valuations needed to be determined for simple objects like furniture and office equipment. I elected to keep my office desk and all the Thomas Mangelson nature photographs in the lower level and fourth floor that I had pledged to St. Vincent Hospital's children's clinic and hospital. In the end, GBHC's and CIC's assets paid off all of our debts.

Dr. Katmeh and I had a limited partnership, Green Bay HeartCare Properties, which owned our building at 1727 Shawano Avenue. New leases with St. Mary's Hospital had to be negotiated for the spaces previously occupied by GBHC and now were transferred to Prevea. Both Prevea and I wanted the merger to be completed in 2007, but the complexity of the various issues, as well as my health challenges to be discussed later, took us into 2008 when the final papers were signed.

While the financial matters were daunting, the outside help from lawyers and accountants proved a significant benefit in that it diminished the psychological impact on me. Nevertheless, the psychological impact became entirely my burden when it came to the transference of GBHC's personnel to Prevea. I knew there would be some degree of duplication of services between GBHC and Prevea following the merger, but was not aware of its extent. GBHC was going to continue to function in our office building on Shawano Avenue, doing what we always did. Some employees stayed while others moved on to new jobs on their own. But when the decision was made to move all of our diagnostic equipment to St. Mary's Hospital for health insurance reimbursement purposes, a number of important positions were eliminated.

One exception was David Miller, our computer expert. Prevea quickly hired him to enhance its existing and expanding software department, which was in the midst of a transition from paper to electronic medical records. Nurses and CNAs (certified nursing assistants) remained needed and quickly made the transfer to Prevea.

There was no eliminated position more devastating to me than my office manager, Sandy Badtke. Prevea simply did not offer her a position. Sandy had been through countless challenges with me for more than two decades. She was the wife of a pharmacist at St. Mary's and originally was recommended to me by Jim Coller as someone looking to expand her management skills. Expand them she did, and in remarkable ways. There were times when Medicare payments were slow, but my employee salaries still had to be paid, either out of GBHC's dwindling cash reserves or my personal bank account. Sandy worked with my long-standing accountant, Kathy Hermans, to create a line of credit from which we could overcome periodic shortfalls in needed cash without invading my personal finances.

Sandy fully understood my vision for Green Bay HeartCare and made sure that all of the employees, at whatever level, understood that vision and lived by it. She spearheaded our recovery from the disastrous flooding event that occurred in our lower-level diagnostic department during a heavy rainstorm, complicated by an obstructed drainage pipe. I was so distraught I could not even go downstairs to look at it, but Sandy completed the supervision of the entire cleanup using multiple recovery agencies. We were able to move back in five months later with the placement of new carpeting and new wallboard. Fortunately, the expensive nuclear cameras were not affected, so we could still do nuclear imaging during the flood. Sandy arranged for the stress portion of the testing to be done on our fourth floor.

Sandy was instrumental in handling the Office of Inspector General's audit of Green Bay HeartCare to be discussed in the next chapter. She made the necessary contacts and appointments with our lawyers from Milwaukee to help me navigate the investigation. This required a clear explanation of GBHC's purpose and methods directed at the prevention of heart disease, as well as the health benefits and cost savings of the early diagnosis of coronary and valvular heart disease.

Sandy was an outstanding manager in so many ways, chief of which was her minimization of my own stress in such issues as: smoothing the integration of Linda Halverson's talents into my vision for stress reduction in our cardiac rehab program; our focus on women and coronary heart disease; and our outpatient stress management program. She managed day-to-day disagreements among employees and hired new nurses like my son, Mark, all of whom clearly understood my vision and were eager to be important contributors to our novel approach to heart disease. She handled salaries and bonuses, and it was her opinion that I relied upon when making adjustments. She was so important to the smooth running of GBHC that we each had cell phones with two lines, enabling her to get my attention any time she felt it necessary.

She was very important in organizing our public relations program and editing our quarterly newsletter. She worked steadily with our marketing firm to make sure our message got out to the public through interviews with reporters or arranging presentations to important community leaders in our fourth floor auditorium. At one point, she arranged for me to be on three different radio talk shows each month in Green Bay, Sturgeon Bay, and Marinette, giving me the opportunity to teach hundreds of patients how to take care of themselves through diet, exercise, and medical management of cholesterol and hypertension, as well as psychosocial management of stress.

One of Sandy's responsibilities was to coordinate our public relations program and expose our special emphasis on prevention to the general public. We conducted three such important programs. The first was the annual Heart Walk. We were responsible for getting this program started, which turned out to be quite a challenge. In spite of our advertising and promotion by the American Heart Association, as well as the presence of one of the local television news anchor women, we had only about five walkers aside from GBHC employees. We gathered on the steps of the Brown County Courthouse in downtown Green Bay and simply walked around Astor Park.

Nevertheless, we persisted until ultimately the event turned into a two-mile walk with hundreds of participants, including teams of walkers who walked in memory of a loved one who had passed away from heart disease. The walk was preceded by encouraging speeches from dignitaries and me, discussing the importance of healthy living. Considerable donations to the American Heart Association resulted.

Our next annual fundraising involvement that Sandy organized was the Heart Association Ball every February, which came to be known as Women's Heart Month. GBHC was a major financial donor, in return

A Life Worth Living

Sandy Badtke (right) was my office manager and an indispensible member of our team at Green Bay HeartCare. She is shown here with Pro Football Hall of Fame member and former Green Bay Packers player and coach Bart Starr in 1999.

for which we received prominent exposure. Sandy even arranged for me to give an interview with one of the TV news anchors. It was a dress-up affair with a silent and an oral auction. In short, it was a big deal and raised a lot of money.

Our third public relations effort was more for the enjoyment of our staff and patients. Sandy worked with Green Bay Packers legend Bart Starr's public relations firm to arrange for him to come to GBHC and meet with the staff for autographs and present an autographed football. He then went to our fourth floor rehab center, where he gave an inspiring speech to our invited guests and complimented GBHC for our vision directed at preventing heart disease, not just treating it.

Unrelated to public relations, but important for GBHC's growth, was Sandy's involvement in putting our research program into action. I had learned from pharmaceutical representatives the need for phase 3 research programs that work with new medications already approved to be safe. Phase 3 studies compare these medications with older medications or treatment protocols to demonstrate that they work incrementally better at preventing or treating certain diseases. I recruited Dr. Thomas Knutson, a family practice doctor, to head this program, and Sandy made all the arrangements to ensure that he received all the government-required education and credentials to supervise our program. I'm proud to say this program continues today under the auspices of Prevea Clinic, and we have been involved in the development of new blood thinners and new cholesterol-lowering agents.

I tried very hard to maintain a position for Sandy at Prevea, including a long discussion with Prevea's president at that time, all to no avail. As the realization sank in that I had no hope of retaining her, I became more stressed than I had ever been in my professional life. GBHC had lost its most important champion of my vision.

An additional heartbreaking loss was that of Amy Eckley, who managed my nuclear department. Because we were handling radioactive materials, we were obligated to follow regulations required by the government's Nuclear Regulatory Commission (NRC). Accurate recordkeeping of our ordering, administration, and disposal of radioactive materials was an absolute requirement for the smooth running of our nuclear stress testing department, as well as the preservation of my nuclear license. Amy provided the necessary recordkeeping and supervision, including the development of manuals addressing proper procedures for dealing with potential radioactive spills, possible incorrect administrations, and guidelines for the protection of our pregnant nuclear technologists.

Amy also kept statistics documenting the accuracy of the physician stress test interpretations, correlating them with subsequent findings on coronary angiography. In addition, she prepared statistics showing equal accuracy of our stress testing conclusions whether the stress test occurred on the treadmill or pharmacologically. On top of these responsibilities, she was a strong partner with Sandy when it came to the development of our women with heart disease program called the Women's Heart Initiative, with its focus on the difficulty many women were going through in their attempts to get physicians to take seriously the possibility that a young woman could have coronary artery disease and not just men.

The difference between the two genders is now known to be in its presentation. The most common presenting symptom for men is chest pain, while in women it is shortness of breath. Each year we would invite one of our women patients to be a guest speaker. They would describe their frustrations as they worked their way through multiple physicians in an attempt to be taken seriously, that just maybe their symptoms might arise from their heart. They would walk us through their experiences before a mixed audience that was eager to learn more about heart disease and its prevention, not just in women but also in men.

One of our speakers actually told a tale of her referral to a psychiatrist to diagnose her symptoms, which were actually cardiac in origin! She eventually made her way to a cardiologist, who identified her heart as the problem and not her head. Her symptoms disappeared after coronary bypass surgery.

Unfortunately for Amy, the merger of Green Bay HeartCare into Prevea did not allow for two nuclear managers in what was now a single nuclear department at St. Mary's Hospital. While Prevea did not have positions for Sandy and Amy, the clinic did have a position for Susie Sutherland, who joined Green Bay HeartCare in Marinette as a registered nurse. Because of her confidence and competence, she subsequently became the manager of the Marinette office in 2002, six years before the merger. Our Marinette office had all the equipment and policies that GBHC had in Green Bay. The presence of multiple regulations, personalities and responsibilities required an on-site manager, and Susie was the perfect person for the challenge. She was an accomplished nurse with a strong knowledge of heart disease and an equally strong desire to organize the Marinette office's policies. Without Susie's managerial skills, not just in cardiology but also in family practice, Prevea would not have kept the Marinette office in the merger. Prevea needed her there as its manager, and it needed a champion who knew the importance of a medical facility in the Marinette region, of which Susie was well aware since she lived in the neighborhood.

She was so important to the smooth running of the Marinette clinic in cardiology and family practice that she continues in a promoted position as Nurse Manager as of this writing, which is approaching two decades since the merger with Prevea. Susie has always cared deeply for her patients and routinely gives them the time they need, answering medical questions and providing strong emotional support. Her most endearing skill is her ability to observe and to learn from what she sees as well as the confidence to ask questions of me when I recommend something she doesn't quite understand.

In fact, for many years I have called her my "Radar," the name of the company clerk in the TV series *M*A*S*H*, who would know what his commanding officer was thinking before he could even put his thoughts into words. By observing me for over twenty years and having seen how I take care of my patients, Susie, like Radar, frequently knows what I am going to recommend to solve a patient's symptoms without asking me, simply waiting for me to confirm what she already knows. If I recommend something out of the ordinary in a complex situation, she will ask me about this unexpected decision. Then, when a similar complexity arises a few weeks or months later, she will remind me of my thought process. Had I not become a doctor, I might have become a teacher, enjoying students like Suzie whose mind was like a sponge, responding to my evolving wisdom. She has absorbed so much of my knowledge that when she becomes concerned about a patient's progress, I become concerned as well.

There were many other devoted employees who made important contributions to GBHC's goals as well as its successes. But much to my chagrin, I could not find openings for everyone in Prevea. They are all sadly missed.

Chapter 28

The OIG

Everyone who remembers the day of John Kennedy's assassination knows exactly where they were when Walter Cronkite announced the news of the event on television. Likewise, I know exactly where I was when I received a call from Sandy Badke informing me of a visit to my office by a detective from Medicare's Office of the Inspector General (OIG). It was 1997. I was in the backseat of a car being driven to my office in Marinette, and we were just passing a new cell tower south of Peshtigo. Sandy told me that the detective had appeared before my secretary the day before, requesting to speak with me. She knew that no one speaks with anyone from the OIG without an attorney present, because the discussion is never about the wonderful job a doctor is doing in his treatment of Medicare patients.

My immediate thought was, "No, this can't be happening to me! What could I have done to warrant a visit from the OIG?"

This news ruined the next several days as I went over and over in my mind what possible misstep I could have committed. Sandy spoke with our advisors at John Goodman & Associates, who gave us the name of a law firm in Milwaukee with attorneys experienced with OIG investigations. They recommended that Sandy call the detective and arrange a meeting as soon as possible at my office with our attorneys present. My anxiety anticipating the meeting, scheduled for the following week, led to several sleepless nights. When the day came, Sandy and two lawyers were sitting on one side of our conference table, the detective and his associate on the other side. I sat at the head of the table between them, waiting to hear the charges.

The first issue involved the two subchapter S corporations for Green Bay HeartCare (GBHC) and Computer Imaging Center (CIC). The OIG office thought I was trying to unbundle charges that should have been included under just one corporation. I was prepared for this question because I was able to describe my frustration with Medicare when I first started submitting bills for patients who were having nuclear stress tests done in my office. When I submitted the proper codes under one account showing that I was billing for both the professional component (my interpretation fee) and the overhead component (my ownership of the equipment with all its attendant costs: depreciation, maintenance, and a dedicated nuclear technologist), Medicare's reimbursement only covered my professional component.

Before initiating my unique outpatient nuclear testing program, which was the only outpatient setting of its kind in the state, the overhead component was always billed by the hospital that owned the equipment. However, I now owned the equipment and was entitled to Medicare's compensation for that ownership. Therefore, to make it clear to Medicare what was going on, I formed CIC, which owned the nuclear testing equipment and billed a separate code for the overhead component from GBHC. It wasn't until I separated the overhead code from the professional code by using two separate corporations that I received the appropriate amount of compensation. I explained my frustration to the detective and my solution for the frustration, which was

A Life Worth Living

perfectly legal. The detective completely understood the need for separate corporations and separate charges.

However, once the OIG finds one problem, they always dig deeper. I waited, therefore, for the next shoe to drop. The detective then told me that the number of nuclear procedures and echocardiograms GBHC was doing was higher than average, and that I would have to produce documentation for the medical necessity for each of these procedures. Otherwise, I would be accused of submitting false claims, called Medicare fraud, punishable by triple damages and even imprisonment.

My anxiety and sleepless nights need no further explanation. A few weeks after this initial interview, I received a list of all the procedures that the government felt were unnecessary because of lack of documentation. My billing department pulled all the charts, which in those days were not computerized. Over several weekends, I reviewed cases of not only my patients, but also of those from my three partners at that time. Some of these patients clearly needed stress tests and echoes with appropriate documentation, but in other cases the documentation was felt by Medicare to be insufficient.

Ultimately, I spent three days in front of an administrative law judge before whom I described additional information not included in the records the OIG had subpoenaed. I was able to satisfy the judge in about forty percent of the cases, but ultimately had to pay back my compensation for the other cases. No further punishment.

On top of the above stress, the OIG also subpoenaed my records for our cardiac screening programs because it thought I was soliciting Medicare patients. I explained that these programs were not specifically directed at Medicare patients, rather at all patients who were concerned about heart disease. Identifying high-risk individuals early allowed me to achieve my goal of preventing heart attacks and decreasing hospitalizations for heart disease by addressing risk factors before symptoms arose. My explanation was accepted, because the financial value of such proactive intervention was obvious, especially with statistics showing that heart attacks were (and still are) the number one cause of death in this country.

The OIG also sent me a subpoena for my congestive heart failure clinic records. I simply explained that CHF is the number one cause of hospital admissions and is also the number one cause of hospital re-admissions. These result from insufficient attention being paid to these patients once they leave the hospital following their initial inpatient care. My extra attention to these patients was GBHC's method of improving the government's own statistics! I had plenty of my own statistics justifying my position and therefore this concern of the OIG was resolved.

My stress during the Medicare investigation took several years for resolution, and was amplified by the fact that I knew my competitors in Green Bay were being interviewed and the word was thus spreading that GBHC was under investigation. This fact was most unsettling because I was really worried that my name and GBHC's name would ultimately be mentioned in the newspaper, announcing to the world the implication that something dishonest was going on under my name. Fortunately, my attorneys convinced the government that I was trying to practice a higher-than-average form of preventive medicine and that there were some unintentional failures in regard to maintaining adequate documentation by my partners and myself. I reimbursed Medicare for the procedures that lacked adequate documentation and, as a result, there was nothing newsworthy to report to the press.

Medicare has a rule that if a medical practice or a hospital is accused of possibly performing unnecessary procedures resulting from poor documentation, either intentionally or unintentionally, the practice is required to demonstrate over a prospective five-year period full compliance with such documentation. A Medicare agent who periodically reviewed us found our documentation so tight and complete that our observation period was reduced from five years to three.

Case closed, but the stress took a while to dissipate because the investigation was taking place while I was working with St. Mary's Hospital to develop and lead its cardiology program. I had made a point of keeping Jim Coller informed of my interaction with the OIG, and I did receive a lot of support from him, which bolstered my confidence.

Now, many years later, this episode with the OIG is only a distant memory, a confirmation of my determination to do what was best for my patients even while experiencing extreme emotional stress of my own. Next, however, physical issues replaced emotional anxiety as my primary source of stress.

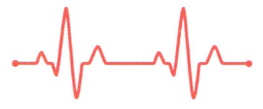

Chapter 29

Internal Challenges

The external challenges I faced while developing the best cardiology practice in northeastern Wisconsin transitioned to physical challenges when I reached my early sixties in the form of lumbosacral disc disease. This condition refers to low back pain caused by a bulging or herniated disc in the spinal column. My problem likely originated from the time I was spending in the cath lab, standing at the side of my patients, struggling to place balloons and stents in narrowed arteries. Interventional cardiology was in its infancy then, and with the equipment available, time was the enemy of the sensitive discs between my lower vertebrae.

It was not unusual for me to spend two to three hours standing and leaning over a patient while I worked to guide the balloon or stent catheter into the region of narrowing. This prolonged standing had a detrimental effect on the discs of my back, an effect which was aggravated by the twenty-five-pound lead apron required to protect my body from the radiation emitted by the X-ray camera. According to Newton's third law of motion, every action has an equal and opposite reaction. In my case, the downward force of my heavy apron created an upward force from the fixed bottom vertebra in my lower back. This led to disc compression and herniation, which squeezed the nerves leading to various segments of my legs.

I went through multiple spinal fusion operations between 2007 and 2014, beginning at the lowest level of my spine and gradually progressing upward. I endured a six-month hiatus at one point due to a staph infection in my back, making me homebound on an IV antibiotic. This experience led directly to my decision to join the Prevea Clinic following my acceptance of the fact that I sadly could never again work in the cath lab.

Dr. Chris VanSaders was successful at fusing each narrowed disc space in my lumbar back, making it possible for me to continue performing coronary angioplasty between operations. When the disc problem entered my thoracic spine, he referred me to Dr. Clifford Tribus in Madison, Wisconsin, for placement of titanium rods and further fusions. My back is now treating me well except when I stand too long or walk too far. I have, therefore, confined my practice to seeing and evaluating patients in the office, continuing my prevention teaching, and enhancing my patients' understanding of why coronary artery disease can progress.

Life was good until 2013, when two seizures knocked me down, one at home in the middle of the night and the second in my office while I was reading echocardiograms. In the latter instance, after my nurses confirmed that I had not experienced a cardiac arrest (what else would anyone think when finding a person lying on the floor in a cardiology office?), they called the rescue squad to take me to the emergency room. I went through an extensive neurologic workup with brain scan, MRI, and EEG, looking for causes of my seizures - all negative. I even went through a sleep study, which also was negative. The final diagnosis was sleep deprivation.

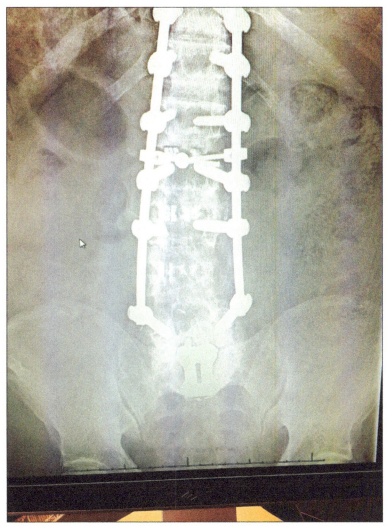
My spine was a wreck after years of performing procedures. This image shows the titanium rods that hold it together.

Now on anti-seizure medication and a better sleep pattern resulting from reduced stress, I have been seizure-free for eleven years and counting. I knew my longevity hinged on taking care of myself if I had any hope of continuing to keep my patients healthy. I knew I had done the right thing when I joined Prevea in 2008. It relieved me of all the management responsibilities that had stressed me at Green Bay HeartCare and transferred them to multiple administrators at the clinic.

I had experienced a good run over the twenty-five years since the birth of Green Bay HeartCare in 1984. It enabled me to accomplished many goals, the chief of which was to increase the average age of my patients from their fifties to their eighties, and to reduce the need for coronary bypass surgery from one hundred percent to less than five percent. With less stress, I sleep better, and with fewer responsibilities, I have reduced my work week from seven days to four.

Now, back to the original query in this memoir: Exactly how did I get here?

Chapter 30

Nature, Nurture, and Determination

What exactly did St. Francis of Assisi mean when he said, "A man who works with his hands, his mind, and his heart is called an artist"? What did he mean by artist? What is art? And what does an artist have to do with the heart? Plato called art a replication of something beautiful or meaningful. The earliest art was concrete, expressed as drawings, paintings, and sculpture, but over time, art took on a more metaphorical definition with the expression of emotion. Still later, centuries later, the principles of art included balance, rhythm, harmony, and unity - a perfect description of the human body. In current vernacular, a person skilled in a particular task or occupation is referred to as an artist in that occupation. Clearly, when St. Francis was using the term "artist," he was referring to just such a skilled individual in the capacity of a physician. He then applied the artistic principles of balance, rhythm, and harmony as a reference to the function of the human body.

Next, the concept of emotion in art led directly to the heart. St.

Francis clearly knew what he was talking about. Thinking back to my discussion of emotional intelligence, I introduced the importance of self-awareness and social awareness. These characteristics are important in determining how we express our native intelligence when confronted with the multitude of challenges in the years ahead. An individual's IQ is only the starting point. How that IQ is molded and expressed is determined by our own experiences (self-awareness) and the influence of others around us (social awareness).

I was smart enough to be valedictorian of my high school class, but not my college class. Yet my experiences early in life, expanded by my professional life, gave me the emotional intelligence to become a successful cardiologist whose patients refuse to allow me to retire. I accomplished my "artistry" by way of my emotional intelligence. I learned about myself from my family, my professors, and my patients. Behind this maturation process was a force called determination. Where did that come from? Reviewing my family's personalities provides an excellent starting point to answer this question.

My grandmother, Bertha, was the first contributor to my determination. She left Budapest with her two sons and supported them in every possible way. She was determined to provide them with opportunities to become well-trained, successful physicians. After they established themselves in their professions, Bertha showered her attention on her five grandchildren: Ian and David in England; Paul, Pat, and me in America.

Although I was never aware of her playing a musical instrument, she loved classical music and passed that love on to me in the literal form of my first classical album: *Beethoven's Violin Concerto in D Major*. She also taught me tolerance (social awareness) through my observation of her ability to balance her love of my father against my mother's romantic love for him, with only occasional flare-ups. I attribute those to the simple recognition that mothers and daughters-in-law do not always see eye to eye. My passive observation of her behavior with my mother taught me there are solutions and compromises that can lead a disagreement toward resolution. In Grandma Bertha's case, separate bathrooms, separate sections of the home, and ultimately separate living abodes were the answers.

I lived through these conflicts and resolutions, learning through observation, and never through inclusion or participation in these disagreements. My father nurtured my determination through his calm perseverance toward his goal of becoming a doctor by outrunning antisemitism in Hungary and Hitler in Germany, traveling through Western European countries, backed by a strong will to ultimately arrive in the United States, where he could develop his passion for psychiatry. All of these tribulations reflect his high score in conscientiousness, which ultimately found its way to me through nature and nurture. I also observed the rise of his social awareness when he calmly handled the conflict between his mother and his wife.

His tendency to focus on goals led to his planting in my mind the seed to apply to Harvard, the best university of which he was aware. When I was a junior at Harvard, I received a questionnaire asking who in my life up to that time had the greatest influence on me. I am not sure what the purpose of this questionnaire was or even what happened to my submission. In any case, my response focused on my mother, simply because she created multiple opportunities for me to demonstrate all of my strengths, which led to my admission to the college of my dreams. In addition, the laid-back subtlety of my father antithetically offset my mother's in-your-face, outgoing personality. I always knew where she stood on any matter. Importantly, I was well-aware of her ongoing search for opportunities for me in music, and the French and Spanish languages.

She enhanced my self-awareness, which engendered considerable self-confidence in me and a willingness to accept risks. In part, this was because she clearly demonstrated her own confidence in me by presenting me with many challenges. She even arranged for my fourth grade teacher to give me extra work during regular class time. Through these opportunities, I rose to become first chair flutist in Maine's all-state band and second chair flutist in the Harvard band. Hearing me practice the flute every day, and knowing my background in the piano, she very quickly concluded that my early flute lessons at the Northern Conservatory of Music in Bangor were too rudimentary. I had already outgrown the instructional skills of my woodwind teacher, who was more experienced with elementary-level music education. She leveraged innovative thought processes to arrange flute lessons for me with a professional flutist, through whose guidance the quality of my flute playing improved immeasurably.

As I look back at what my mother did for me and what I expressed in that Harvard questionnaire, I can credit her with the following statement: "A conscientious personality without the finest opportunities is a personality unfulfilled." To a great extent, I owe my self-awareness to my mother. It was a key foundational piece in my ability to develop emotional intelligence. Her determination to provide me with these opportunities pales when I compare it with her determination to do battle with none other than the United States Army. The story goes as follows:

My mother, Rita, on her 75th birthday on February 4, 1995

When my father enlisted in the army as a psychiatrist in 1946, the requirement for a physician was a three-year tour of duty. A benefit of this commitment was the allowance of the physician to take his family along with him to his assigned base, which in my father's case happened to be Puerto Rico, the landing site of soldiers who were dealing with "shell shock," what we now call post-traumatic stress disorder (PTSD). It was a reasonably comfortable assignment for my father to treat these psychiatrically disabled soldiers while surrounded by his wife and two little boys, ages three and one. During the first year and a half in Puerto

Rico, the military reduced the requirement for physician enlistment from three years to two. So, at the two-year mark in 1948, my mother took my brother and me home to Binghamton, New York, expecting my father to be following shortly behind. However, for some reason, his discharge papers were held up – no husband and no father to join my mother and her two boys in Binghamton.

Her determination to set the army straight went into high gear. She wrote to and called the Department of the Army, and in no uncertain terms informed the top brass of the fouled-up paperwork. She was bound and determined not to be by herself with two little boys, now ages four and two, living in a small apartment along with her mother-in-law, Grandma Bertha. You know from my previous reports what that relationship could be like.

Thanks to my mother's badgering, the US Army belatedly saw things her way, and only a few weeks later my father was in Binghamton, his discharge papers in hand! Rita versus the US Army? No contest!

The nurturing and determination I gained did not end with my mother. I could not have reached my full level of social and self-awareness without my wife. Kathy is endowed with the same determination as everyone I have described, but her determination was fostered by a completely different set of circumstances that began during her youth. She had the self-awareness to recognize that she was better off dealing with and adjusting to her mercurial mother rather than engaging with social services. Becoming a foster child simply was not an option. She had her own high level of emotional intelligence to succeed in high school, develop the self-confidence to leave her mother's influence, and become a first-grade teacher after graduating from the University of Maine with a degree in education.

After we married, she was determined to create the closely knit family of her dreams, which had sustained her all the while she was struggling through her chaotic childhood. Kathy did everything she could to help me reach my ideal practice of cardiology. She took care of every aspect of our home life, repeating what she had observed in Grandma Bertha and my mother, and created a loving environment for our three

Our boys in 1992 - From left, Mark (19), Scott (21), and Todd (17)

boys, Scott, Mark, and Todd, as well as for me. I would be present at most of their soccer games, but Kathy was there for all of them, even though the only soccer word she understood was "GOAL!!!!"

Beside her loyal presence at soccer matches, Kathy rewarded the team with her culinary invention, banana chocolate chip cookies, as a reward for a game well-played, even when the final score was not in their favor. Her family focus extended to our home life, where she did everyone's laundry, ironing, cooking, transportation, and cleaning so that I could not only conduct a successful practice in Green Bay, but also expand it to Marinette and beyond. She made sure our boys were expanding their own personalities, talents, interests, and compassion, allowing them to thrive with their own evolving emotional intelligence promoted through four generations of native intelligence. We passed down our determination to our sons, who also had strong emotional intelligence and were supported by their wives, Sarah, Andrea, and Christina, to help them achieve their goals.

Scott's determination directed him to excel as a soccer goalkeeper, becoming varsity goalkeeper on his high school team that won the Wisconsin private schools state championship in his senior year. He then was a walk-on varsity goalkeeper at the University of Rochester, and following graduation, played semi-pro soccer and taught youngsters the art of protecting the net. Scott graduated with an economics degree from the University of Rochester. He has focused on executive compensation, first as an analyst, and subsequently progressing to the level of vice president for executive compensation and talent at CF Industries, a global manufacturer of products for clean energy and emissions abatement.

Mark's determination led him to nursing where, following college graduation from the University of Rochester, he graduated first in his class from Bellin College of Nursing in Green Bay. He then received a master's degree in nursing as an Advanced Practice Nurse Practitioner (APNP), giving him the opportunity to apply the same nurtured, compassionate, and empathetic care practiced by his forefathers. Mark has always had an artistic bent, which found its expression in culinary ex-

Our family at Mark's graduation in 1996. From left are my mother Rita, Kathy, Todd, me, Scott, and Mark.

Future cardiologist Todd was a daredevil at age 10. He practiced even riskier stunts than this while I was at work! Recall my father's concern about me playing baseball catch the morning of my piano recital. That was pretty tame by comparison.

ploration, developing and perfecting unique combinations of ingredients.

Todd's determination always was directed toward healthcare. He graduated from Harvard College with a degree in biology and a goal of entering the field of orthopedics upon enrolling at the University of Michigan Medical School. His interest in orthopedics was stimulated by his tennis success in high school, ranking number nine for boys singles in the state of Wisconsin and number two in doubles. However, orthopedics lost its appeal early in his medical school experience and was replaced by cardiology. He became certified in interventional cardiology, placing stents in locations which I used to see only in my dreams. Outside his passion for medicine, Todd has become enthusiastic about, and intensely involved in, marathon running.

The nature and nurture from my parents also extended to my brother Paul and sister Pat, both finding their own niches in healthcare. Paul went to Bowdoin College in Brunswick, Maine, and received his medical degree from Chicago Medical School. He practiced primary care in the Boston area for more than thirty-five years before retiring. Pat graduated from Tufts College in Massachusetts with a degree in psychology. She helped displaced workers rediscover their footing and find new positions during the stressful recession of the early 2000's.

We have all been able to balance our career passions with strong outside interests to achieve a nice equilibrium in our lives. For Scott, it was soccer; for Mark, adventures in cooking; for Todd, long distance running; for Paul and his wife, Nancy, travel and friendships; for Pat and her husband, Bill, tennis and travel to Hawaii; for me, the piano, flute, and vintage wine collecting; and for Kathy, ad hoc cooking and children's activities such as "Next Door Theater," of which she was secretary. We have enjoyed strong support and devotion from our spouses, without whom there would be no passion of any kind.

Nature as a foundational force

Most of my comments regarding nature have focused on nurture and the way it shapes our personalities and interests. In regard to nature, my emphasis has been primarily on intelligence, which then can be molded and expanded by our experiences of everyday life – our personal environment (nurture). Now I would like to discuss another aspect of nature unrelated to intelligence, namely artistry; not in St Francis's terminology, but in the broader context of talent in the specific art of music.

In just my own family, there is evidence of a clear genetic transmission (nature) other than intelligence that is focused on true art. It is not a one-to-one transmission from family to family, but rather a more random selection, scattered among individuals with similar, but not identical genetic material. Let's start with Grandma Bertha. She did not play a musical instrument, but she loved classical music, which eventually was passed down to me. It was also passed down to my father, whose classical music gene was attached to an advanced piano playing gene.

Next, the love of classical music and the dexterity of playing the piano and later the flute came down to me. My ability to play the flute may have been genetically passed on to me from my uncle, Bertha's other son, Paul. Meanwhile, my dedication toward piano artistry was passed on to Mark's daughter, Sophia, and son, Owen, who further expanded his musical interest to the ukulele. My father's piano interest was passed through my sister to her son, Paul, who is proficient in the piano and the guitar.

A separate, genetically determined interest is demonstrated by my appreciation of fine wine, which has passed down to Scott, but not Mark or Todd, nor to my sister Pat or brother Paul. However, it did find its way to Pat's son, my nephew Paul. Furthermore, the degree of interest in any skill can be enhanced by nurture. For example, the difference between a concert pianist and a social pianist is, to a great extent, determined by nurture, which can stimulate the necessary determination to practice sufficiently to reach a very high degree of dexterity. It can lead to performing in concert halls in front of thousands of listeners, contrasted with a lower degree of determination aimed at adequate satisfaction from just playing in front of family and friends. Complicated concepts, but interesting to ponder.

This complexity is addressed by author David McCullough in his nonfiction book, *The Wright Brothers*, which focuses on nature, nurture, and determination. In fact, on the title page of the first chapter, he quotes Wilbur Wright, who concisely describes these characteristics as follows: "If I were giving a young man advice as to how he might succeed in life, I would say to him, pick out a good father and mother, and begin life in Ohio." He was saying, in effect, success starts with the genes of our parents and then flourishes with the determination nurtured by our environment, our family, our friends, and our teachers, who for the Wright brothers happened to be in Ohio. In spite of naysayers, Wilbur and Orville were determined to find a way for humans to fly like the birds. They saw no reason such a goal was unattainable. If birds

Our Green Bay family on the occasion of my eightieth birthday

can do it, we should be able to find a way to do it as well.

The Wright brothers spent several years observing and studying the aerial characteristics of numerous types of birds to learn about the mechanics of flying. They used their intellect to understand the importance of airflow against the wings of the birds. They employed the calculations of physics, focused on the Bernoulli principle, to create a motorized, two-winged aircraft in 1903 that could fly in figure-eight patterns carrying two adults. They were clearly poster brothers for the power of determination nurtured by those around them, even assisted by advice from their competitors in the field of flying, competitors who had not reached the same level of understanding as the Wright brothers themselves.

My determined goals even before arriving in Green Bay were to prevent heart disease and decrease the number of open-heart surgical procedures. In my gradual move toward these goals, I began by entering the bodies of my patients with balloon and stent catheters through the femoral artery. Now fifty-four years into my practice, I still enter the bodies of my patients, but my entrance is through their ears with words of knowledge, comfort, caring, and encouragement. As I walked down the hospital hallway those many years ago, I was starting to feel I had combined all of St. Francis's attributes of an artist, but realized at the same time I needed the force of determination to make that spark of artistry flare brightly enough to allow me to navigate my way through the challenges I have described. Assistance along this pathway came by way of nature (my inherited intelligence), nurture (my father's medical instincts of psychiatry), Grandma Bertha's unrelenting perseverance, my mother's intense determination to find opportunities, and my wife's selfless, enduring love.

As I enter my eighties, I have analyzed thousands of patient experiences and learned that the heart has its own language with many dialects. They vary from individual to individual, with such words as tightness, fullness, shortness of breath, dizziness, palpitations, weakness, tiredness, jaw pain, toothache, arm pain, wrist pain, even ear pain, etc. — all accompanied by body language such as clenched fist, tears, restlessness, fear, frustration, and many more. I have learned to translate the language of the heart and created multiple substrates contributing to my gradual development of the wisdom of the Greeks. This allows me to make the following conclusions regarding what patients really want from their doctor:

- They want to be cared for and not just treated.
- They want to feel safe, not in danger.
- They want to be in control and not just passive observers.
- They want to be listened to and not just heard.
- They want to be educated and not just informed.
- They want to feel trust and not uncertainty.
- AND ABOVE ALL, THEY WANT TO FEEL HOPE.

Through my experiences over the past five-plus decades, and through the support of my ancestry family as well as my current family, I have risen to the level of St. Francis's term of "artistry," beginning in Bangor, Maine, far from the Wright brothers' home in Dayton, Ohio. Aside from our differing locations, we both succeeded in soaring to unprecedented heights. Now, centuries after St. Francis, I can face my patients and say, "I'VE GOT THIS!"

Epilogue

Breaking Walls

Marcus Fabius Quintilianus was an educator who lived between 35 and 100 A.D., and often spoke in hyperbole. One of his more lasting statements was as follows: "If there is no doorway, one must break through the wall." Over the course of my career in cardiology, I have found many opportunities to create new openings, following the teachings of Fabius Quinilianus and my mother.

Looking back, I am proud to have many firsts attached to my cardiology practice and business. These stem from a determination to succeed and an entrepreneurial spirit that many healthcare practitioners do not possess. For example:

I was the first cardiologist to introduce M-mode echoes and then two-dimensional echoes in 1975; I was the first cardiologist in Green Bay to perform coronary angiography on a patient during an active heart attack, sending him directly to the operating room for coronary bypass surgery after visualizing a severely narrowed right coronary artery; I was the first cardiologist to open an independent cardiology practice outside a hospital; I was the first cardiologist to purchase their own echocardiogram machine, exercise treadmill, and nuclear camera for diagnosing heart disease outside a hospital in a standalone outpatient cardiology clinic; I was the first cardiologist to open an independent cardiology office in Marinette, Wisconsin, offering echoes, nuclear stress tests, laboratory studies, EKGs and outpatient cardiac rehabilitation.

At our Marinette grand opening, I became the first cardiologist to receive a key to the city of Marinette, presented to me by the mayor; I was the first cardiologist to introduce an annual Women's Heart Initiative, offering a platform for me to discuss the differences between men and women with heart symptoms, highlighted by women who, in their own words, spoke of their own frustrations to be taken seriously by their healthcare providers; I was the first cardiologist to offer mobile echocardiograms transported to neighboring hospitals that could not afford the expensive equipment themselves; I was the first cardiologist to offer mobile nuclear equipment in a remodeled large box truck, which allowed performance of nuclear stress testing in the truck simultaneously while two other patients were being tested in the office.

I was the first cardiologist to extend our advertising to free T-shirts with our printed logo, "Good for Life," given to all patients after a stress test; I was the first cardiologist to give employees, as Christmas gifts, logo-inscribed gym bags, beach blankets, and polo shirts; I was the first cardiologist to offer a weekend retreat to beautiful Door County, Wisconsin, for all office employees and their families, focused on group cohesiveness as well as empathy for our patients with heart disease; I was the first cardiologist to talk about the heart on radio talk shows, including four stations every month, taking calls from listeners and answering questions about heart disease; I was the first cardiologist to open an office in Sturgeon Bay (Door County), seeing cardiac patients in the office, preceded by a forty-five minute radio broadcast.

I was the first cardiologist to focus their practice on prevention; I was

Kathy and I enjoy some ice cream cones in 2022.

the first cardiologist to grade their partners on how well they were helping patients reach their cholesterol goals; I was the first cardiologist to move his offices to west Green Bay across the street from St. Mary's Hospital, expanding the availability of heart care to west Green Bay and further north; I was the first cardiologist to work with St. Mary's Hospital to develop a west side catheterization lab, breaking the east Green Bay monopoly; I was the first cardiologist to use CT calcium scoring to identify high-risk patients for potential heart attacks before developing symptoms.

In providing advice to patients who wish to prevent coronary artery disease or have been working to recover from a coronary artery disease event, I have found myself repeating the following statements many times:

- "Good health does not happen by accident."
- "If you could choose only one intervention to protect your heart

Kathy and me at a Green Bay HeartCare event in the late 1990s.

and your brain, it should be to engage in exercise, which has the downstream effect of lowering the bad cholesterol, raising the good cholesterol, lowering blood pressure, lowering blood sugar, reducing weight, and on top of it all, making people feel better about themselves both physically and emotionally."

- "Stay off the roof and ladders."
- "Do things more slowly than you did twenty years ago. You may look twenty years younger than most, just don't act it!"
- "If you are on blood thinners and hit your head when you fall, go to the emergency room for a CT scan of your head to make sure there's no bleeding into or around your brain."

- "Twenty-five percent of people over the age of sixty-five experience a fall. Don't be one of them."
- "Our culture is not known for its patience; so, if you become sick or experience an orthopedic injury, give yourself plenty of time to recover. Statistics have shown that if a person over the age of sixty-five requires forty-eight hours of bed rest in the hospital, it takes three months of physical therapy to recover what you lose in those forty-eight hours."
- "When you get up in the morning, sit on the edge of your bed for twenty to thirty seconds to avoid dizziness if your blood pressure falls when you stand up."
- "Take your medicine with a routine activity so you don't forget."
- "Controlling cholesterol is the easiest and most effective risk factor adjustment I can provide."
- "Twenty-five percent of people who experience a heart attack or sudden death have no prior symptoms. If someone you know has multiple risk factors for coronary artery disease, especially a family member who had a heart attack at a young age, let me know because I can prevent it in them."
- "The best way to manage your congestive heart failure is to weigh yourself every day. If your weight goes up by two to three pounds a day for two days or more in a row, call me. You may be developing congestive heart failure."
- "If you experience any discomfort above your diaphragm with exertion, or more than your usual shortness of breath with any particular activity, call me."
- "Now that you have a new stent in your coronary artery, we need to make sure your risk factors become even better so you don't need another one."
- "The secret to longevity is to live long enough for technology to catch up with your needs."
- "If somebody gives you good news, don't ask any questions."
- And finally, "I have no plans to retire!"

As a result of following these words of advice, my patients live longer, oftentimes outliving anyone else in their family. The current average age of my patients is seventy-eight years versus sixty-five when I started in 1975.

Yes, A LIFE WORTH LIVING!

Acknowledgements

No physician has the opportunity to practice the specialty they love without the help of their nurses. I have mentioned two of these nurses in my narrative: Betty Stevens and Susan Sutherland, whose outstanding contributions led to the formation of Green Bay HeartCare. I need to add several additional nurses and emergency medical technicians (EMTs), without whom I would not be where I am now.

Abby Lynch RN is so confident and reassuring with my patients that they feel they are actually talking to me when they call to describe their symptoms or concerns. Abby always discusses these concerns with me, and in the process has learned a great deal about taking care of problems related to heart disease. She always quickly returns their calls and satisfies their concerns with my recommendations. I also could not do without Julie Klika, who has worked with me for twenty years. She advises my many patients who take a blood thinner called Coumadin, which needs regular, careful monitoring. Julie has seen extreme lab results at the low end and the high end, and without input from me (except in the rarest circumstance), knows exactly what to do with the aberrant results.

Kelly Prokopovitz is an EMT on Prevea's cardiology staff who also works as a first responder with the rescue squad. In our office, she checks patients into the exam room, determines their vital signs, confirms their medications, and goes over their chief complaints. She is upbeat, funny, and keeps the mood of the clinic light and sparkling. She loves her cellphone camera, which she has used to create larger-than-life photographs of herself and me, which are attached to the wall in my office. I therefore cannot possibly forget who she is and, for that matter, who I am! When I first met Kelly, I told her that her Irish first name did not fit with her Polish last name. So I renamed her Kelly Rose O'Malley — which she regularly uses as her cellphone ID.

Prevea Heart has another EMT with Prevea responsibilities that are similar to Kelly's, but whose primary work is with the fire department. Her name is Gabrielle Gallert, whose nickname, Gabby, has always captured my fancy. I told her that, as fate would have it, another Gabby had appealed to me many years ago, when I was only six years old. This Gabby (no physical comparison!) was the bearded sidekick of my favorite cowboy, Hopalong Cassidy. To distinguish my new EMT version, I call her "Mon ami Gabbi."

Carol Mijal RN fills in for Abby when my telephone calls tighten Abby's schedule. Her main responsibility is the unenviable task of controlling my son Todd's busy schedule, both in the office as well as the cath lab. As a result, scheduling conflicts are a regular part of her daily activity.

Samantha Lewins RN checks patients in and out, as well as fields patient questions over the telephone. Her primary contribution to the clinic is her amusing photography, dressing the staff to mimic cartoon characters. I will always remember her favorite sandwich: grilled cheese with peanut butter!

Last, but not least, is Brad Lepinski RN, who at one time managed our entire nursing staff. The interpersonal challenges, however, were frustrating and prompted him to do what he loves, which is just being a nurse and taking care of patients. His idiosyncrasy is the use of the floor around his desk as a filing system for his paperwork. Or maybe these papers are simply a boundary to keep others away from him? Brad won't say! When he is not working, he has tweaked his culinary skills to create the best tiramisu I have ever tasted.

No medical office can run efficiently without good managers for oversight and problem solving. Prevea Cardiology is fortunate to have two such supervisors in Chris Hudson and Becky Clisch. Without these managers, paperwork would not be completed, conflicts would not be resolved, questions would not be answered, and absences would not be filled.

I am deeply indebted to Mike Dauplaise and Bonnie Groessl from M&B Global Solutions Inc. for their expertise and advice, without which the conversion of my words into this book would not have been possible.

And before these words even landed on paper, they required the skill of my transcriptionist, Laura Herlache, to whom I will be eternally grateful for her accuracy, and especially for the patience required while we fine-tuned our new transcription equipment.

About the Author

Healthcare has been in Dr. Peter Fergus's professional genes since birth. His father was a psychiatrist, his mother a psychiatric nurse. His paternal uncle was a pulmonologist whose son was a gastroenterologist. Dr. Fergus's brother was an internist, and his sister a psychologist. Two of Dr. Fergus's sons are in healthcare, one as a cardiologist, the other a nurse practitioner.

During Dr. Fergus's youth, his father frequently described the many opportunities that exist in healthcare: multiple medical specialties, teaching opportunities, and research options. Therefore, there was little doubt that he would become a doctor, but what specialty?

The answer to this question arose from a Boston City Hospital attending cardiologist who was exceptionally stimulating, engaging, and charismatic. From that

I am a big fan of lemon meringue pie, especially the meringue!

meeting in 1972, when Dr. Fergus was a senior resident at the hospital, he knew he wanted to be a cardiologist. His post-graduate training involved the Boston University Service at Boston City Hospital and the Harvard Service at West Roxbury VA Medical Center, the referral center for all veterans with heart disease from northern New England. He served six years in the Massachusetts Army National Guard during his internship, medical residency, and cardiology fellowship in Boston, where he was a captain of a medical company consisting of five corpsmen attached to an artillery battalion.

Dr. Fergus moved his family from Boston to Green Bay, Wisconsin, following his education in medicine and heart disease to develop a practice devoted to the treatment of heart disease. After nine years of getting to know the medical needs of Green Bay and its surrounding regions, he saw multiple opportunities to form his own cardiology practice. He founded Green Bay HeartCare to expand the treatment of heart disease well beyond the borders of Green Bay and far into the northern portions of Wisconsin and Michigan's Upper Peninsula. This expansion culminated in a second office in Marinette, Wisconsin, one hour north of Green Bay.

Dr. Fergus still sees patients in Green Bay, and even those from the far north, some of whom are willing to drive two hours or more to Marinette to seek his advice on how to maintain a healthy heart.

Made in the USA
Monee, IL
23 December 2024